Recipes from an
Italian Terrace

VALENTINA HARRIS

Recipes from an Italian Terrace

For Joce, with all my love and much more. Memories are made of this.

Acknowledgments: A huge thank you to Camilla Stoddart for all her enthusiasm, energy and fun. Thank you also to Robin for stepping in, and to everybody who modelled so beautifully for Sam! And, of course, my village and all my neighbours, now indelibly recorded for posterity. And finally, thank you to Martin Pettinger for creating such beautiful vessels in his pottery, especially for this book.

First published in Great Britain in 2004 by
Cassell Illustrated
A division of Octopus Publishing Group
2–4 Heron Quays
London E14 4JP

Text copyright © 2004 Valentina Harris
Design and layout © 2004 Cassell Illustrated

A CIP record for this book is available from the British Library.

Commissioning Editor: Camilla Stoddart
Editor: Robin Douglas-Withers
Art Director: Jo Knowles
Designer: Austin Taylor
Photography: Sam Bailey
Cooking: Ross Forrester
Entertainment: Joce Berg

ISBN 1 84403 056 3

Printed in China

NOTES

1 wine glass is the equivalent of 100 ml (3 ½ fl oz).

The most common Italian bread is ciabatta, but any fresh, crusty bread will do.

Eggs are medium in size unless stated otherwise.

Parmigiano Reggiano is a hard, Italian grating cheese, usually referred to as Parmesan.

contents

introduction

I wrote this book imagining myself on the terraces at my cookery school in Tavernelle, surrounded by family, friends and guests, enjoying that most Italian of sensual experiences – eating outside in glorious surroundings, when the air is warm and balmy and the atmosphere congenial.

I have one outstanding memory of an outdoor eating experience, on a warm June night on the terrace by the babbling stream, with the whole valley lit up by thousands of brilliant, twinkling fireflies. The magic of that evening will never leave me, the food was delicious, the wine heady and the laughter infectious, but the setting itself was truly unparalleled. I have never seen fireflies in that number. They were literally everywhere, and there were so many of them that our candles were almost superfluous. Against a background of such stunning, shimmering activity, we all felt enormously privileged to be there and I know we all still remember it well.

The idea of the recipes in this book is simple: to help you to create dishes that are easy to prepare, reliant as ever upon the best available fresh ingredients, and that will help you to enjoy memorable, delightful meals outside, whether you are in Italy or not.

Eating outside in Italy is an activity that takes place from the very beginning of summer, right through to the last few hours of the season, when summer slides itself lazily back into autumn. Erroneously, people refer to it as eating al fresco, but, in fact, eating al fresco means eating in a cool place, in the shade, preferably under a shady pergola, but never in the full sunshine of the middle of the day. For an Italian, eating and drinking with the sun beating down on your head and the table is tantamount to suicide! There are special tablecloths and tableware reserved for eating outside, and all Italians, even those with the tiniest outdoor space, know the joys of eating good food in the open air. And of course, there are special recipes for such occasions too.

Eating outside is always much less formal than eating in the dining room, so the food offered tends also to be less formal and much less complicated. It is the sort of food which can be eaten with your fingers, which can be lingered over unhurriedly and savoured languorously. Hot days and sultry nights create an atmosphere of their own, when there is less desire than ever to spend too long slaving over a hot stove, and appetites tend to be less voracious — the opposite of wanting the rib-sticking, satisfying dishes of the winter season.

The collection of recipes that follows reflects these feelings. They are, almost without exception, recipes that hold special memories for me, as they are dishes that I have enjoyed at least once when outdoors and mainly in Italy. All of them are hopefully relaxed and as easy going as possible – it should be far too hot to get too wound up or agitated. This is not to say, of course, that you cannot transport them indoors, and enjoy them at any time of the year! It is also my hope that some of them will become firm favourites with you and your family and friends.

I wish you all many happy hours of cooking and eating, whether you are on your own Italian terrace or at the kitchen table, or on my terraces with me at Villa Valentina. As with all of my books, it is always my intention to bring a little corner of authentic Italy to you, all you have to add are the ingredients and your own special touches.

Buon Appetito!

Valentina

1.

small titillations
ANTIPASTI

Literally translated, the word 'antipasti' means 'before the meal', so by definition, this is always a small light course. Traditionally, it would precede pasta, risotto, soup or gnocchi, but with smaller appetites these days, it usually replaces either the 'primo' or the 'secondo'.

Originally, bruschetta was simply sliced bread that had been lightly rubbed with garlic, sprinkled with olive oil and then dusted with salt and pepper. In Tuscany it was known as fett'unta (oily slice). Crostini used to mean pâté: it was the original recipe for a purée of cooked liver, seasoned with capers, wine, carrots, celery, onions, butter and parsley. It is said that this was the pâté recipe transported to France by Caterina de Medici upon the occasion of her marriage and subsequent French residence.

plain bruschetta and crostini
bruschetta e crostini

serves 4

8 slices ciabatta or other crusty Italian bread
3 garlic cloves, peeled
extra virgin olive oil
sea salt and freshly ground black pepper

method

Heat the grill and toast the bread on both sides until just coloured. Lightly rub each sides of the toast with the garlic. Drizzle or brush over some olive oil and season.

Arrange the bruschetta on a platter and sprinkle with the remaining olive oil.

To make crostini (smaller-sized servings), cut the bread into bite-sized pieces before adding the oil and serving. Crostini are not usually rubbed with garlic.

This old and traditional Sicilian recipe makes the most of the island's favourite vegetable: the aubergine. To really develop the flavours, make this the day before. It is lovely as a topping on crostini or bruschetta, or inside warmed focaccia.

aubergine and olive bruschetta
bruschetta con la caponata

serves 6

1 kg (2¹/₄ lb) aubergine, cubed
sea salt
100 ml (3¹/₂ fl oz) extra virgin olive oil
40 g (1¹/₂ oz) onion, chopped
250 g (9 oz) assorted pickles, such as
onions, peppers, gherkins
25 g (1 oz) capers, rinsed and dried
6 celery sprigs, chopped
50 g (2 oz) green olives, stoned
1 tbsp granulated sugar
1 wine glass red wine vinegar
2 tbsp pine nuts
10 slices ciabatta or other coarse
Italian bread, toasted on both sides
2 garlic cloves, peeled
extra virgin olive oil
5 tbsp fresh ricotta

method

Sprinkle the cubed aubergines with salt, put them in a colander in the sink and leave them to drain out their bitter juices. Leave for about 1 hour (longer if possible) then wash and dry thoroughly.

Divide the oil between two deep pans. Fry the aubergine cubes in one pan, and the onion, pickles, capers, celery leaves and olives in the other, over a low heat, for about 15 minutes.

When the aubergine is soft and well-coloured, remove it from the pan oil and leave to drain on kitchen paper.

Add the sugar and vinegar to the onion mixture and let the vinegar fumes evaporate before stirring in the aubergine and the pine nuts.

Rub the toasted ciabatta lightly with the garlic and then drizzle over some olive oil. Spoon over the onion and aubergine mixture, then top with a spoonful of ricotta and serve.

My favourite vegetable rides again, this time on top of deliciously garlicky toast. If time is short, you can throw a jar of drained, chargrilled artichokes preserved in oil into the food processor. Once reduced to a chunky purée, add mint, cream and seasoning to taste.

artichoke bruschetta
bruschetta di carciofi

serves 4

1 lemon
4 large globe artichokes
3 tbsp extra virgin olive oil
2 garlic cloves, very finely chopped
10 fresh mint leaves, chopped
3 tbsp double cream
sea salt and freshly ground
black pepper

FOR THE BRUSCHETTA
8 slices ciabatta or other crusty
Italian bread
3 garlic cloves
extra virgin olive oil

method

First, cut the lemon in half and squeeze the juice into a bowl of cold water large enough to hold the prepared artichokes. Drop the squeezed lemons into the bowl.

Next, prepare the artichokes by stripping and trimming them and discarding all the leaves. Cut each stripped artichoke into quarters and remove the chokes with a teaspoon. Drop the artichokes into the bowl of water.

Pour the olive oil into a pan, add the chopped garlic and heat until sizzling.

Drain the artichokes and add them to the pan. Stir carefully then add enough water to just cover the vegetables. Simmer gently for about 1 hour or until completely softened and almost falling apart. Stir occasionally and check the moisture level to stop the pan from drying out.

Towards the end of the cooking time, prepare the bruschetta. Brown the bread on both sides, preferably over a wood fire, then rub the garlic over the hot toast, pressing hard if you want it very garlicky or gently if you want a more subtle flavour. Drizzle each slice of toast with the olive oil.

Stir the mint, cream and seasoning into the pan. Heat through and then spoon generously on to the bruschetta.

My second favourite vegetable also makes its way lusciously on to bruschetta! During asparagus season, my local market in La Spezia offers asparagus in all shapes, sizes and colours, including plump purple and ivory pale varieties.

asparagus bruschetta
bruschetta d'asparagi

serves 4

1 bunch asparagus spears
extra virgin olive oil
8 slices ciabatta or other crusty
Italian bread
3 garlic cloves
sea salt and freshly ground
black pepper

TO GARNISH
extra virgin olive oil
balsamic vinegar
shavings of Parmigiano Reggiano

method

First, prepare the asparagus by snapping off the hard woody bases about halfway down the spears.

Arrange the asparagus over a hot barbecue, brushing them with the olive oil and sprinkling with salt and pepper. Grill until soft, continuing to brush with oil and turning frequently so the asparagus does not burn.

Meanwhile, prepare the bruschetta. Brown the bread on both sides, preferably over a wood fire, then rub the garlic over the hot toast, pressing hard if you want it very garlicky or gently if you want a more subtle flavour. Drizzle each slice of toast with the olive oil.

Arrange the cooked asparagus on the prepared bruschetta. Sprinkle with the balsamic vinegar and garnish with shavings of Parmigiano Reggiano, then serve immediately.

The delicious combination of flavours and textures in this traditional Tuscan speciality has remained popular throughout many generations in Italy. You can also use this topping as a dressing for pasta, or on top of a plain Risotto alla Parmigiana, or eat it cold when on a picnic.

squid bruschetta
bruschetta di totani

serves 4

450 g (1 lb) baby cuttlefish or squid
100 ml (3^1/$_2$ fl oz) extra virgin olive oil
^{1}/$_2$ wine glass white wine
300 g (10 oz) passata
1 kg (2^1/$_4$ lb) fresh spinach
2–3 garlic cloves, halved
1 dried red chilli pepper
4 large slices Italian bread, such as
Casareccio or Pugliese
sea salt
2 tbsp chopped fresh flat leaf parsley,
to serve

method

Clean the fish carefully, removing the ink sac and hard beak. Cut off the tentacles then slice the body section of the squid into 1 cm (^{1}/$_2$ inch) strips.

Pour half the oil and all of the wine into a large pan then add the passata and the fish. Simmer over a gentle heat for about 20 minutes, stirring frequently. When the fish is tender, season it with salt.

Meanwhile, boil or steam the spinach until it is wilted, then drain and, when cool enough to handle, squeeze it between your hands to remove as much water as possible. Chop coarsely and set aside.

Heat the remaining oil in a pan with the garlic and chilli. Add the spinach and the fish. Toss everything together and heat for about 10 minutes, stirring constantly. Remove the garlic and the chilli.

Lightly toast the bread then top generously with the squid mixture. Sprinkle with the parsley and serve at once.

A delicious Italian version of mushrooms on toast. If you add a slug of brandy while cooking the mushrooms it will enrich their flavour. You can also make the dish more substantial by either adding a slice of prosciutto to the topping or laying a poached or fried egg on top of the bruschetta. For extra flavour, why not try shaving Parmigiano Reggiano over the cooked mushrooms just before serving. And if you want something really filling, you could try all of the above!

mushroom bruschetta
bruschetta di funghi

serves 4

8 large slices crusty Italian bread
2 tbsp unsalted butter
450 g (1 lb) mushrooms, thinly sliced
2 garlic cloves, crushed to a smooth purée
3 tbsp single cream
3 tbsp finely chopped fresh flat leaf parsley
a little extra virgin olive oil, for brushing
sea salt and freshly ground black pepper
fresh rosemary sprigs, to garnish

method

Toast the bread on both sides then brush with the oil and keep warm. Meanwhile, gently melt the butter in a frying pan, over a medium heat. Add the mushrooms and garlic and cook, turning frequently, for about 10 minutes.

Season to taste then stir in the cream and parsley. Spoon the mushrooms mixture on to the toasted bread and serve at once, garnished with a sprig of fresh rosemary.

For this topping to be really tasty you need to use tomatoes that are truly sweet and juicy and packed with flavour. Hence, I have given you the option of using canned tomatoes, which must be of really good quality and not watery or bland. For added tomato taste, you can squeeze a little concentrated tomato purée into the mix.

bruschetta with tomatoes and red onions
bruschetta con pomodoro
e cipolle rosse

serves 4

5 tbsp extra virgin olive oil
1 large red onion, coarsely chopped
10 very ripe fresh tomatoes
4 large slices ciabatta bread, or other
coarse Italian bread
1 garlic clove
sea salt and freshly ground
black pepper

TO GARNISH
chopped fresh flat leaf parsley
8 thin slices red onion

method

Heat three-quarters of the oil in a frying pan then add the onion and fry gently for about 10 minutes, stirring frequently.

Meanwhile, prepare the tomatoes. If you are using canned tomatoes, they simply need to be drained and coarsely chopped. If you are using fresh tomatoes, first blanch them in boiling water for about 1 minute then, when cool enough to handle, skin, seed and chop coarsely.

Add the tomatoes to the onions and season with salt and pepper. Heat through while you prepare the bread.

Heat the grill and toast the bread on both sides until just coloured, then lightly rub both sides with the garlic. Arrange the bread slices on a platter and sprinkle with the remaining oil.

Spoon the hot tomato and onion mixture over each slice of bread, sprinkle with parsley and lay 2 slices of raw onion on top of each bruschetta. Serve immediately.

These crostini make either a wonderful starter or delicious bite-sized snacks if cut smaller. The salad is very pretty and combines a lot of wonderful flavours. If you want even more stunning colours, use blood oranges when they are available.

For an alternative flavour, try using walnut oil instead of olive oil or make the crostini with walnut bread instead of ciabatta. If you don't like walnuts, add half a very finely sliced leek to the salad and leave out the nuts altogether.

gorgonzola and nut bruschetta with radicchio salad
bruschetta di gorgonzola e noci con insalata di radicchio

serves 4

2 heads radicchio
2 oranges, peeled and thinly sliced
8 tbsp extra virgin olive oil
1 loaf ciabatta, neatly sliced
1 garlic clove, peeled
150 g (5 oz) Gorgonzola cheese
10 walnuts, shelled and coarsely chopped
sea salt and freshly ground black pepper

method

First, make the salad. Wash and thoroughly dry the radicchio. Separate the leaves and arrange on a flat serving platter then scatter the orange slices over the leaves. Sprinkle with a little of the olive oil and season lightly with salt and a generous grinding of black pepper. Set aside until required, but for no longer than 30 minutes, otherwise the leaves will go limp and soggy.

Discard the two ends of the loaf (you could use them to make breadcrumbs). Arrange the slices of bread on a grill pan and brown on both sides until crisp and warmed through. Rub lightly with the garlic.

Meanwhile, mash the Gorgonzola with a fork until smooth. When the bread is ready, brush each slice lightly with the remaining olive oil.

Spread all the slices evenly and generously with the mashed Gorgonzola and sprinkle each one with the chopped walnuts. Arrange on the bed of salad and serve at once.

The word prosciutto in Italian simply means ham and in Italy it will either be prosciutto crudo (cured ham) or prosciutto cotto (cooked ham). The very best prosciutto crudo comes from the Langhirano Valley outside the city of Parma where the climatic conditions are perfect for curing ham.

crostini with Parma ham and mozzarella
crostini di Prosciutto di Parma e mozzarella

serves 6

12 slices ciabatta bread
12 slices Parma ham
12 slices mozzarella cheese
about 2 tbsp extra virgin olive oil

method

First, put the bread on a grill pan and toast on both sides until lightly coloured.

Remove the grill pan from the heat and arrange a slice of ham on each crostini, folding it over towards the centre of the bread so that it fits neatly on each slice. Next, place a slice of mozzarella on top of the ham.

Slide the crostini back under the grill and toast until the cheese has melted and is slightly browned. Brush with olive oil and serve at once.

Deliciously creamy toppings like these are fabulous spread over crunchy, toasted ciabatta or served as dips. They can even be used to dress pasta and are lovely to take on a picnic, especially one with a fire for toasting bread over. Sometimes I use the mixture in sandwiches. Try the pepper mixture with avocado and bacon, or cured ham.

pepper and aubergine crostini
crostini alle melanzane e peperoni

serves 4

1 large red pepper
1 large aubergine, halved
1 hard-boiled egg
1 tsp mild mustard
10 large capers, rinsed and chopped
1 fresh red chilli, chopped
8 slices crusty Italian bread
3 tbsp extra virgin olive oil
sea salt and freshly ground black pepper
3 tbsp chopped fresh flat leaf parsley, to garnish

method

You can either grill or bake the pepper and aubergine.

To grill, put the pepper and aubergine under a medium grill or on to a barbecue and cook, turning frequently, until soft.

To bake, place them on a baking tray and bake for 30 minutes in an oven preheated to 200°C (400°F) Gas 6.

Set the grilled or baked vegetables aside until cool enough to handle, then skin and deseed the pepper and remove all the softened pulp from the aubergine.

Put the pepper in a food processor with the egg and the mustard. Season with salt and pepper then whizz until smooth. Transfer to a small bowl and set aside.

Wash the food processor jug, then add the aubergine pulp, the capers and the chilli. Season with salt and pepper then whizz until well combined and smooth.

Toast the bread on both sides until lightly coloured then brush with the oil. Spread one half of the bread with the pepper cream and the other half with the aubergine cream. Sprinkle with the parsley and any remaining oil and serve.

So pretty! So very green! You can use vegetables instead of the squid – for example, 3 large chargrilled peppers – or poached fish if you prefer. This terrine is especially delicious when made with squid chargrilled on the barbecue and chopped into small chunks. You can also make the terrine using red pesto and prawns, or carefully filleted and boned poached red mullet.

pesto terrine
terrina al pesto

serves 4

1.25 kg (2³/₄ lb) squid
1 carrot, cut into small chunks
1 celery stick, cut into small chunks
1 onion, sliced
5 sheets gelatine
5–8 tbsp pesto, depending upon the intensity of its flavour
sea salt and freshly ground black pepper

method

Clean the squid thoroughly and place it in a pan with the vegetables and enough water to cover. Bring to the boil and simmer gently for about 1 hour or until completely cooked and softened.

Drain, discarding the vegetables. Chop the squid coarsely when cool enough to handle.

Line a 450 g (1 lb) loaf tin with clingfilm. Soak the sheets of gelatine in enough cold water to cover it generously for 20 minutes or until softened, then melt it in 3 tablespoons of boiling water over a very low heat.

Put the pesto into a small bowl then add the gelatine and stir together. Pour three quarters of the pesto into the lined loaf tin and put in the fridge until it has set (about 1 to 2 hours).

Meanwhile, keep the remaining pesto as liquid as possible by keeping it warm (place a thick cloth around the base of the bowl) and stirring continuously.

When the pesto in the loaf tin has set, add the squid, pressing it down very firmly into the pesto and making quite sure there are no air pockets. Add the seasoning, and pour the rest of the pesto into the tin so it completely covers the squid. Cover the tin with foil and place a weight on the top. Refrigerate for at least 2 hours.

To serve, remove the weight and the foil and gently turn out the terrine. Remove the clingfilm and slice thickly. Delicious served with cold boiled potatoes, dressed with a drizzle of olive oil.

This is one of those fabulously versatile recipes that can be used either as a dip, a spread for crostini or bruschetta or as a sauce for pasta. You can either use artichokes preserved in olive oil or fresh ones, which you will need to prepare and cook yourself – which is, of course, considerably more laborious! When cleaning and preparing artichokes, trust your fingers to guide you as to what to turn away. If it feels rough or sharp to touch, your mouth will react the same way!

artichoke pâté
crema di carciofi

serves 4–6

4–6 globe artichokes, preserved
or fresh
1 lemon, halved
extra virgin olive oil
2 tbsp mascarpone cheese or thick
double cream
2 garlic cloves
juice of ½ lemon
a large handful fresh flat leaf parsley,
stalks removed and chopped
2–3 tbsp freshly grated
Parmigiano Reggiano
sea salt and freshly ground
black pepper

method

If using fresh artichokes, begin by stripping away all the coarse outer leaves until you reach the soft, pale interior. Cut the artichokes in half and carefully extract all the threads. Run your fingers over the artichokes so you can find and then trim away any remaining rough patches.

Rub the artichokes with the lemon halves then drop them into a basin of cold water. Squeeze the lemon juice into the water to prevent them from oxidising.

When you are ready to make the pâté, drain the artichokes and braise them in a little olive oil and water until they are soft. Allow them to cool before using.

Put the artichokes, mascarpone or cream, garlic, lemon juice, parsley and Parmigiano Reggiano into a food processor and whizz until blended but not smooth. Season to taste, then transfer into a small serving bowl, cover with extra virgin olive oil and use as required.

Make sure the prosciutto is perfect and freshly sliced. Use Prosciutto di Parma, Prosciutto di San Daniele or Prosciutto di Carpegna for the best result. Alternatively, for a very lightly smoked flavour, choose a high-quality speck. Buy a melon that is ripe and juicy – preferably the orange-fleshed and slightly-scented Charentais or Cantaloup variety. When in season, you can also add green or black figs.

classic antipasto
antipasto classico

serves 4

1 ripe melon, weighing about
1.25 kg (2³/₄ lb)
2 handfuls mixed salad leaves
750g (1 lb 10 oz) *prosciutto crudo*,
thinly sliced

method

Cool the melon in the refrigerator. When you are ready to serve, slice and seed it and arrange it on a platter on top of the salad leaves. Arrange the prosciutto slices languidly in the centre of the dish and serve at once.

This is a delectably messy dish that requires everyone to use their fingers in order to really enjoy the prawns. Fingerbowls or a nearby water source are a real must. Only use prawns that are large enough to peel easily and not so small and fiddly that they drive everybody mad. You can eat these hot or cold, and, of course, you can add chilli to the garlic if you want an extra kick.

prawns in tomato sauce
gamberoni al pomodoro

serves 6

1 kg (2¼ lb) large raw shell-on prawns

5 tbsp extra virgin olive oil

3 garlic cloves, chopped

250 ml (9 fl oz) passata

10 fresh basil leaves, torn into small pieces

sea salt and freshly ground black pepper

method

First, give the prawns a quick rinse in cold water and pat them dry.

Heat the olive oil in a large, deep frying pan then add the garlic and fry over a gentle heat for about 5 minutes. Add the passata and stir, then cover and simmer for a further 5 minutes.

Add the prawns and season generously with salt and pepper. Stirring constantly, cook the prawns over a high heat for about 5 minutes, depending upon their size.

Cover with a lid and remove the pan from the heat. Leave to stand for about 3 minutes, then tip out on to a platter, sprinkle with the basil and serve either hot or at room temperature depending on your preference.

Carpaccio consists of very finely sliced raw beef or veal, originally created at the Cipriani in Venice many decades ago. The name Carpaccio refers to the painter of the same name whose works were exhibited in Venice at the time. The colour of the dressed raw meat reminded the cook at the Cipriani of the colours used in the artist's paintings.

If you don't feel confident about cutting the meat so finely, you can always ask a friendly butcher to do it for you.

carpaccio with a tuna sauce
carpaccio tonnato

serves 4

3 courgettes, sliced lengthways into ribbons with a potato peeler
400 g (14 oz) beef fillet, sliced paper thin
2 tbsp mayonnaise
2 tbsp plain yogurt
juice of ½ lemon
50 g (2 oz) canned tuna in oil
sea salt and freshly ground black pepper

method

Blanch the courgette ribbons in boiling salted water for 1 minute then plunge them into iced water. Drain and pat dry carefully. Arrange the courgette ribbons and the sliced beef on 4 individual plates.

Put the mayonnaise, yogurt, lemon juice and tuna in a food processor and whizz until smooth. Season then pour over the sliced meat and courgettes. Chill until required.

These lovely little lemony meatballs make perfect canapés, and, served cold, are a perfect addition to a picnic.

They can also be used in the Timballini di Pasta (see page 68), or can be made larger, and after sealing in oil can be slowly stewed in tomato sauce. The mixture will also work for a tangy meat loaf.

lemon meatballs
polpettine al limone

serves 6

400 g (14 oz) minced veal or beef or turkey or chicken

100 g (3½ oz) fresh breadcrumbs

3 tbsp chopped fresh flat leaf parsley

100 g (3½ oz) grated Parmigiano Reggiano

3 large eggs

½ wine glass cold water

juice of ½ lemon

grated zest of 1 lemon

5 tbsp fine dry breadcrumbs

sunflower seed oil, for deep-frying

sea salt and freshly ground black pepper

method

Put the meat, fresh breadcrumbs, parsley and cheese with 1 of the eggs in a large bowl. Season then mix together very thoroughly until all the ingredients are well combined.

Blend in the water gradually so that the liquid can be evenly absorbed and, finally, mix in the lemon juice and zest. Mix with your hands for a few minutes more then shape the mixture into small balls about the size of a cherry.

Beat the remaining 2 eggs in a separate bowl then dip the meatballs first in the beaten egg and then in the dry breadcrumbs. Heat some oil in a deep frying pan and fry the balls for a few minutes until crisp and browned, turning frequently.

Drain the balls thoroughly on kitchen paper and either use in the Timballini di Pasta or serve as canapés.

This delectable combination of flavours and textures never fails to remind me of summer days in Italy. Cleverly, Italian supermarkets all sell neatly sliced and perfectly griddled frozen aubergines. Not only are they delicious but they also cut out a lot of the work for this dish! You can also use potatoes, courgettes or artichoke hearts or a combination of them all. Plenty of crusty bread for mopping is essential.

baked aubergines with tomato and mozzarella melanzane alla parmigiana

serves 4

2 long aubergines
3 tbsp extra virgin olive oil
250 ml (9 fl oz) ready-made or
homemade tomato sauce
(*see page 61*)
125 g (4 oz) mozzarella, sliced
100 g (3½ oz) freshly grated
Parmigiano Reggiano
about 15 fresh basil leaves, shredded
with your fingers
sea salt and freshly ground
black pepper

method

Cut the aubergines into disks and discard the ends. Sprinkle with salt and lay in a colander. Place a plate directly on top of the aubergines and put a weight on top so it presses down on to them. Stand the colander in the sink for 1 hour while any bitter juices drain away.

Preheat the oven to 200°C (400°F) Gas 6 and lightly grease an ovenproof dish or baking tin with a little of the olive oil.

Rinse and pat dry the aubergines slices then brush lightly with the remaining oil. Grill the aubergines on both sides until soft and slightly browned.

Next, start to fill the dish or tin, adding the salt and pepper as you go along. Put a layer of tomato sauce in the bottom, then add a layer of aubergine slices, a layer of mozzarella slices, another layer of tomato sauce, a sprinkling of Parmigiano Reggiano and a few torn basil leaves. Repeat until the dish or tin is full, finishing with a thick layer of tomato sauce, Parmigiano Reggiano and basil.

Bake in the oven for about 30 minutes. If your layers fill the dish or tin, place it on a baking tray to catch any drips. Remove from the oven and leave to stand for about 5 minutes before spooning out to serve.

There are two ways of cooking this dish: on a barbecue or in the oven. If you want to cook the pepper boats on the barbecue, you need to grill the peppers before you stuff them. You can also make the stuffing in a pan heated on the barbecue. If you decide to cook the stuffed peppers in the oven, simply stuff the uncooked peppers with the filling and bake them.

yellow pepper boats
barchette di peperone giallo

serves 4

4 small yellow peppers, halved and deseeded

6 tbsp extra virgin olive oil

1 garlic clove

4 anchovy fillets preserved in olive oil, drained

150 g (5 oz) coarse Italian bread, cubed

1 aubergine, cubed

2 tbsp chopped fresh flat leaf parsley

sea salt and freshly ground black pepper

method

To cook on a barbecue, settle the peppers on the grill and cook until just softened, turning frequently.

Meanwhile, pour half the oil into a pan and fry the garlic until it has browned, then discard.

Stir in the anchovy fillets and cook until they have melted into the oil. Add the bread and stir until coated, then remove the bread and put it to one side.

Add the remaining oil to the pan along with the aubergines and cook until softened. Return the bread to the pan and heat through, stirring continuously for a few more minutes and adding a little water to prevent sticking. Season thoroughly, then add the parsley and stir.

When the peppers are soft, fill them with the aubergine and bread stuffing and serve.

To bake in the oven, first preheat the oven to 180°C (350°F) Gas 4. Prepare the filling as above then simply fill the uncooked peppers and place them on a baking sheet. Bake in the oven for 30 minutes or until the peppers are soft and cooked through. Serve immediately.

An attractive and refreshing way to serve this delectable cheese. You can vary the filling if you wish and use a smoked fish of your choice. What is essential is that you use buffalo mozzarella, which is almost useless for cooking with, and that it should be incredibly fresh and moist. I like to use smoked mackerel or other fish with a really strong taste, although smoked salmon, as used in the picture on the opposite page, also works.

stuffed mozzarella
mozzarella farcita

serves 4

4 fresh buffalo mozzarella, weighing 250 g (9 oz) each

100 g (3½ oz) smoked fish, cooked and flaked or chopped

3 celery sticks, very finely chopped

4 tbsp extra virgin olive oil

sea salt and freshly ground black pepper

celery leaves, to garnish

method

Cut each ball of mozzarella into 4 thick slices, starting from the base and working to the top.

Mix together the fish, celery and half the oil. Season to taste then spread the mixture between the mozzarella slices, reconstructing the cheeses as you go.

Drizzle the stuffed cheeses with the remaining oil, sprinkle with salt and pepper and scatter any remaining filling around the sides of the mozzarella. Chill until required or serve at once, garnished with the celery leaves.

A great classic: delicious and wickedly rich! This is probably the closest thing to what the Americans call French Toast, only with added flavour and no cinnamon. For this recipe you need plain, square, white bread called Pane in Cassetta in Italian.

mozzarella in a carriage
mozzarella in carrozza

serves 4

8 slices white bread
1 tsp anchovy paste or sun-dried tomato paste
8 thick slices mozzarella
3 eggs, beaten
olive oil, for frying
sea salt and freshly ground black pepper

method

Make the bread into sandwiches using a little anchovy or sun-dried tomato paste and using the mozzarella as a filling. Firmly push down on each sandwich with the heel of your hand so it is tightly pressed together.

Beat the eggs in a bowl and season with the salt and pepper. Turn the sandwiches in the egg mixture so they are completely coated. Leave to soak until you are ready to fry them.

Heat a frying pan on the hob or on the grill of a barbecue. When it is hot, drizzle a little oil into the pan. Carefully remove the sandwiches from the egg mixture and lay them in the hot pan. Fry them on both sides for 3–4 minutes, or until golden and crisp. Serve at once.

A very simple but delicious Campanian speciality that is light enough to follow with a pasta course, or fantastic just on its own. Make as one big frittata or as several individual ones. Serve it with a crisp green salad or a tangy tomato and oregano salad and a loaf of crusty bread. Great on picnics too, as it is delicious served cold.

frittata with mozzarella
frittata di mozzarella

serves 4

8 large eggs
250 g (9 oz) mozzarella, cubed
1 tbsp milk
2 tbsp chopped fresh flat leaf parsley
or basil leaves
3 tbsp extra virgin olive oil
sea salt and freshly ground
black pepper

method

Beat the eggs in a large bowl then add the mozzarella, milk and herbs. Season to taste and stir everything together until it is well combined.

Heat the oil in a 20 cm (8 inch) frying pan until sizzling hot then pour in the egg mixture. Pull the mixture into the centre, rotating and turning the pan so that the egg sets and browns on the underside.

After about 5 minutes, or when the mixture feels firm and reasonably set, turn over the frittata by placing a large plate on top of the pan and turning the pan upside down so that the frittata falls on to the plate with the cooked side uppermost. Carefully slide the frittata back into the hot pan with the cooked side on top and the uncooked side underneath.

Shake the frying pan to settle the contents and cook the frittata for a further 3–4 minutes. Slide the frittata out of the pan on to a clean serving plate and serve hot or cold.

A very intensely flavoured and robust frittata (omelette) that is perfect for anyone who loves the salty, fishy taste of anchovies. It is perhaps a good idea, when preparing a picnic or buffet, to serve a slightly less salty and aggressive tasting frittata alongside this one.

frittata with anchovies, tuna and parmigiano
frittata di acciughe, parmigiano e tonno

serves 4

200 g (7 oz) fresh anchovies
3 tbsp dry breadcrumbs
6 eggs
1 tbsp freshly grated Parmigiano Reggiano
1 tbsp chopped fresh flat leaf parsley
50 g (2 oz) canned tuna in olive oil, drained
3 tbsp extra virgin olive oil
sea salt and freshly ground black pepper

method

Preheat the oven to 180°C (350°F) Gas 4.

Wash and thoroughly drain the anchovies. Pat them dry carefully. Remove the head, spine and innards from each fish.

Divide the anchovies into two equal piles. Coat one pile of fish in the breadcrumbs ensuring that each anchovy is thoroughly covered. Coarsely chop the other pile of fish.

Beat the eggs in a large bowl and season with salt and pepper. Add the Parmigiano Reggiano, parsley, tuna and the chopped anchovies.

Thoroughly grease an ovenproof dish with the olive oil then pour in the egg mixture. Arrange the breadcrumb-coated anchovies on the top and bake in the oven for 20–25 minutes or until golden brown and cooked through. Serve warm or cold.

Frittata, or omelette, is always welcome at picnics and summer buffets or even as a sandwich filling. Beloved by all Italians, it is made in a wide variety of shapes, sizes and thicknesses, depending on the occasion! Be careful not to add too much cheese to the mixture as it might make it stick to the pan.

spinach frittata
frittata di spinaci

serves 4–6

2 kg (4½ lb) fresh spinach
6 eggs, beaten
3 tbsp freshly grated Parmigiano Reggiano
4 tbsp extra virgin olive oil
sea salt and freshly ground black pepper

method

Steam the spinach until it is soft and wilted. Drain, and when cool enough to handle, squeeze out any excess moisture with your hands. Chop finely and put into a large bowl.

Add the eggs to the spinach with the Parmigiano Reggiano and mix well. Season to taste.

Heat the oil in a wide, shallow frying pan and when it is very hot, pour in the egg mixture. Shake the pan to flatten and even out the frittata and cook until the underside is browned and firm.

Place a large plate over the pan and turn the pan upside down so the frittata falls on to the plate, cooked side up. Carefully slide the frittata back into the pan with the uncooked side underneath. When the underside has cooked and the frittata is firm, turn it out on to a large plate. Serve hot or cold.

A lovely fresh-flavoured starter that is ideal for summer. It is inspired by the perennially popular Italian pizza, but is a bit more sophisticated. Use tartlet cases with fluted edges to make them look really pretty. To garnish, you could use sprigs of fresh basil and some very tiny cherry tomatoes. If you decide to make your own pastry, add a little freshly grated Parmigiano Reggiano into the dough for an extra kick of Italian flavour. If you would like a stronger tasting dish, use a little pesto instead of, or as well as, the Parmigiano Reggiano.

tomato tartlets
tartine al pomodoro

serves 6

1 packet frozen puff pastry

1 garlic clove, finely chopped

3 tbsp extra virgin olive oil

1 x 400 g (14 oz) can chopped tomatoes

a handful of fresh basil leaves, torn into small pieces

250–300 g (9–10 oz) fresh mozzarella, finely cubed

2 tbsp freshly grated Parmigiano Reggiano

unsalted butter, for greasing

sea salt and freshly ground black pepper

method

Preheat the oven to 180°C (350°F) Gas 4. Grease and line six 10 cm (4 inch) loose-bottomed tartlet tins.

Roll out the pastry to a 3 cm (1¼ inch) thickness and cut into 6 circles large enough to line the tartlet cases. Press the pastry gently into place, then prick the bottom of the pastry with a fork. Place a piece of baking parchment over the base of each tartlet and weigh down with baking beans.

Bake the tartlets in the oven for about 10 minutes. Remove the baking beans and lining paper. When the tartlets are cool, take them out of their cases and place them on a baking sheet.

In a small pan, fry the garlic in the olive oil for about 5 minutes, then pour in the tomatoes. Turn up the heat and cook the sauce quickly for about 5 minutes, stirring frequently. As soon as the sauce looks glossy take it off the heat. Season to taste and stir in the basil. Set aside until needed.

When you are ready to serve, preheat the grill until it is very hot. Divide the tomato mixture evenly between each of the pastry cases then add the mozzarella. Sprinkle each tartlet with a little Parmigiano Reggiano, then slide the baking sheet under the grill for about 2 minutes, or until the mozzarella is just beginning to melt and the tops look golden. Serve immediately, as if you fill the pastry cases too long before you want to serve, the pastry may become very soggy.

2.

pasta etc.
PRIMI PIATTI

The course that traditionally follows a light antipasto is called primo *and will always be either pasta, risotto, gnocchi or soup. This is usually considered to be more important than the main course (secondo) which follows. In order for the meal to be balanced it is vital that this course, whatever it is, comes between the* antipasti *and the main course so that it is not out of place in a traditional meal.*

For those summer days when you crave pasta but don't want to get hot and bothered in the kitchen, this hot pasta with its fresh sauce and chilled ricotta is both wonderfully satisfying and cooling.

pasta for the summer
pasta d'estate

serves 4

2 garlic cloves, crushed to a purée

½ tsp sea salt

freshly ground black pepper

7 tbsp extra virgin olive oil

1 heaped tbsp chopped fresh flat leaf parsley

750 g (1 lb 10 oz) fresh, ripe, juicy tomatoes

1 sweet red onion, very finely chopped

1 ripe avocado, peeled and cubed

a handful of fresh basil leaves, torn into pieces with your fingers

400 g (14 oz) spaghettini

4 tbsp fresh ricotta, thoroughly chilled

method

Mix the garlic, salt and pepper together then stir into the olive oil. Add the parsley and leave to stand.

Prepare the tomatoes by immersing each one in a bowl of boiling water for 1 minute then removing the skin.

Cut the skinned tomatoes in half and remove all the seeds. Chop the flesh into small cubes and stir into the garlic and olive oil mixture.

Add the onion, avocado and basil leaves and stir very thoroughly.

Leave the sauce to stand for up to 5 hours, or until you are ready to dress and serve the pasta.

When you want to eat, bring a large pot of salted water to a rolling boil and throw in the pasta. Stir, cover and return to the boil. Cook until tender but firm to the bite, then drain and return to the cooking pot.

Pour the sauce over the pasta and mix together thoroughly. Transfer to 4 individual plates, spoon over the ricotta and serve.

For this dish, I like to use a fish that can withstand a fairly long cooking time without losing all its flavour and texture. I have opted for swordfish, which remains firm, and cod, which flakes well, so there are two completely separate textures within the same dish. However, you can use any combination of fish you like or even use squid if you prefer. Parmigiano Reggiano is rarely served with fish pasta dishes, hence its absence here.

pasta with a fish sauce
pasta al sugo di pesce

serves 6

2 garlic cloves, thinly sliced

2–3 tbsp chopped fresh flat leaf parsley

$1/4$ dried red chilli

3 tbsp extra virgin olive oil

1 swordfish steak weighing about 75–100 g (3–3$^1/_2$ oz), cubed

2 cod fillets weighing about 180 g (6$^1/_2$ oz), cubed

2–3 tbsp dry white wine

300 ml ($^1/_2$ pint) passata

550 g (1$^1/_4$ lb) pasta of your choice

sea salt and freshly ground black pepper

2 tbsp chopped fresh mint, to garnish

method

In a large pan, very slowly fry the garlic, parsley and chilli together in the olive oil. When softened add all the fish and fry for about 3 minutes.

Add the wine and stir for about 2 minutes until the alcohol has boiled off. Next, add the passata and stir thoroughly, then season and cover. Simmer for about 15 minutes or until the sauce is thick and glossy.

Meanwhile, bring a large pot of salted water to the boil then add the pasta. Bring the water back to the boil and cook the pasta until tender, then drain and return to the pan.

Pour the sauce over the pasta, sprinkle with the mint and toss everything together very thoroughly before transferring to a large dish and serving immediately.

Although I am not that fond of coloured pasta, I do think the green and the black varieties look dramatic and taste good too. The black pasta used for this dish is made from cuttlefish ink, which gives it its jet-black colour when cooked and its strong fishy taste. It perfectly complements the delicate scallops and sharp lime flavours in the sauce. If you prefer not to use the corals, then simply discard them. Otherwise, add them to the dish at the last possible moment so they only just cook through and turn opaque.

black pasta with scallops and lemon
pasta nera con le capesante al limone

serves 4

extra virgin olive oil

10 fresh scallops

2 lemons

350–400 g (12–14 oz) black, cuttlefish ink pasta

sea salt and freshly ground black pepper

a large handful of chopped fresh flat leaf parsley, to serve

method

Heat a frying pan until it is piping hot. Brush with a little olive oil and sear the scallops for 2 minutes on each side. Zest and juice the lemons and reserve.

Bring a large pan of salted water to the boil, toss in the pasta and stir. Cook until al dente, then drain thoroughly. Return the pasta to the hot pan.

Add the scallops, the zest and juice of the lemons and about 4 tablespoons of olive oil. Season to taste with salt and pepper. Return the pan to the heat and turn the mixture quickly for about 1 minute to heat it through.

Transfer to a warmed serving dish and sprinkle with the parsley before serving.

When I am in Italy, I make this recipe with the octopus I buy from one of the many fish vendors at the market in La Spezia. But octopus is rather harder to come by in the UK so I have opted for squid instead.

linguine with squid
linguine allo scoglio con la seppia

serves 4

400 g (14 oz) fresh tomatoes
3 garlic cloves, chopped
6 tbsp extra virgin olive oil
1 tsp concentrated tomato purée
550 g (1¼ lb) fresh squid, sliced
1 wine glass dry white wine
1 dried red chilli, finely chopped
375 g (13 oz) linguine
sea salt
3 tbsp chopped fresh flat leaf parsley, to serve

method

Drop the tomatoes into boiling water for 1 minute. Drain and, when cool enough to handle, skin and chop the tomatoes very roughly.

Put the garlic and oil into a large pan and heat until sizzling. Add the tomatoes and tomato purée and stir for a few minutes.

Next, add the squid. Cook for 1 minute to seal the fish then add the wine. Allow the alcohol to evaporate before reducing the heat. Add some salt and a chopped chilli to taste. Cover and simmer very gently for about 1 hour or until the squid is very soft.

Towards the end of the cooking time, bring a large pan of salted water to the boil then add the linguine and cook until al dente. Drain the pasta then return it to the hot pan. Dress with the sauce then turn out on to individual plates or a large serving dish. Scatter over the chopped parsley and serve immediately.

Pesto is one of the most traditional tastes of Italian summer time! In my opinion, it is especially delicious with pasta and fish. The traditional way to serve it is with pasta, green beans and potatoes, mixed together in equal parts. This recipe is a development of that principle. Any fish will work fine, though obviously the texture will alter depending upon which fish you choose. If you prefer, you can add fish that has been barbecued, then broken up and mixed in with the remaining ingredients.

orecchiette with potatoes, fish and mangetout
orecchiette con patate, pesce e taccole

serves 4

1 carrot, chopped

1 onion, chopped

1 celery stick, chopped

3 tbsp extra virgin olive oil

450 g (1 lb) filleted fish of your choice, cut into chunks

½ wine glass dry white wine

200 g (7 oz) potatoes, peeled and cubed

300 g (10 oz) orecchiette pasta

100 g (3½ oz) mangetout

4–6 tbsp homemade or ready-made pesto

sea salt and freshly ground black pepper

method

Fry the carrot, onion and celery together with the oil until the vegetables are soft. Add the fish, cover with the wine and cook together for about 6 minutes or until the fish is cooked through.

Bring a large pan of salted water to the boil, add the potato and cook for about 5 minutes, then add the pasta and continue to boil.

Three minutes before the end of the cooking time, add the mangetout.

Drain and transfer back into the saucepan, add the fish and the pesto, season and mix thoroughly together. Serve at once.

Most pasta dishes use ready-made fresh or dried pasta. But here, because a sheet of pasta is needed, you will have to make your own. This unusual fish roll takes a little more effort, but the results are well worth it. Make sure you don't let the roll sag into the water while it cooks.

fish-filled pasta roll
rotolo di pasta al pesce

serves 6

FOR THE FILLING
400 g (14 oz) cooked white fish, skinned and flaked
a small bunch of mixed herbs
150 g (5 oz) raw prawns
1 tbsp unsalted butter
1–2 tbsp plain flour
1 tsp lemon juice
½ tsp grated lemon zest
2 tbsp freshly chopped fresh flat leaf parsley
sea salt and freshly ground black pepper
fresh pasta (see page 61)
tomato sauce, to serve (see page 61)

method

First, cook the white fish by placing it in a pan of water with the bunch of herbs and some light seasoning. Simmer until the fish is just tender, then remove it with a slotted spoon and set aside to cool.

Add the prawns to the pan and cook until they turn pink. Drain, reserving the cooking liquor.

Next, make a béchamel sauce, by melting the butter in a small pan then adding enough flour to make a thin paste. Add the reserved fish cooking liquor a little at a time, mixing it in until the sauce resembles a runny béchamel.

Flake the white fish, removing any small bones and skin. Shell the prawns and chop coarsely.

To make the filling, put the fish, prawns, 8–12 tablespoons of the béchamel, the lemon juice and zest, parsley and seasoning in a large bowl and mix until well combined. Set aside until required.

Make the pasta as described on page 61 and roll it into a sheet of about 20 x 30 cm (8 x 12 inches). Spread the filling over the sheet, keeping within 2.5 cm (1 inch) of the edges. Roll up the pasta like a Swiss roll, working from the short end and ensuring there is no air between each turn of the spiral. Wrap the fish roll tightly in a clean muslin cloth and tie the ends securely.

Bring a fish kettle of salted water to the boil and carefully slide the wrapped roll into the water, taking care not to let it sag in the centre. Boil gently for about 1 hour, then remove carefully and drain.

Unwrap the muslin, lay the roll on a board and cut it into slices with a sharp knife. Arrange on a plate and spoon over a little tomato sauce.

fresh egg pasta
la sfoglia

serves 4

450 g (1 lb) plain white flour
a pinch of sea salt
5 eggs

method

Pile the flour into a bowl or the centre of a large, clean pastry board. Add a pinch of salt. Make a dip in the centre and break in the eggs. Gradually, mix together the flour and the eggs, working the flour into the eggs from the centre.

Eventually, a thick dough will form. Add more flour if the consistency is too wet. Begin to knead the dough, pressing it away with the palm of your hand and then folding it back over itself.

When it is soft and elastic, leave it to rest for 20 minutes before using.

tomato sauce
sugo al pomodoro

serves 4

2 tbsp extra virgin olive oil
1 garlic clove, crushed
1 onion, finely chopped
400 g (14 oz) canned tomatoes, chopped
1 tbsp tomato purée
2 tbsp chopped fresh flat leaf parsley
sea salt and freshly ground black pepper

method

Heat the oil in a large pan and gently fry the garlic and onion until transparent and soft.

Add the tomatoes and tomato purée and season to taste. Simmer gently over a low heat for about 20–30 minutes or until the sauce is rich and thick.

Add the chopped parsley and serve.

This delicious mixture of fresh and sun-dried tomatoes makes a lovely sweet-flavoured sauce that is perfect with any shape of pasta. The addition of the ricotta at the very end adds a lovely creamy and slightly granular texture to the overall dish. You can, of course, offer Parmigiano Reggiano separately at the table if you wish.

pasta with sun-dried tomatoes and ricotta
pasta con pomodori secchi e ricotta

serves 4–6

6 tbsp extra virgin olive oil
1 small onion, finely chopped
1 celery stick, finely chopped
1 anchovy fillet, drained, rinsed and chopped
250 g (9 oz) sun-dried tomatoes preserved in olive oil, coarsely chopped
300 g (10 oz) tomatoes, skinned, seeded and coarsely chopped
450 g (1 lb) dried pasta
3 tbsp fresh ricotta
2 tbsp chopped fresh flat leaf parsley
sea salt and freshly ground black pepper

method

Gently warm the oil in a pan then add the onion, celery and anchovy and fry until the vegetables are soft.

Add the sun-dried tomatoes to the pan and fry very gently for a further 5–10 minutes then add the fresh tomatoes. Stir, cover and simmer gently for about 20 minutes, or until the sauce is thickened and glossy.

Bring a large pan of salted water to the boil. Tip in the pasta, stir and return to the boil. When the pasta is ready, drain quickly and return to the saucepan it was cooked in.

Pour the sauce over the pasta, toss together thoroughly and add the ricotta and a little pepper.

Toss again, then tip out on to a serving platter or into a warmed pasta bowl, or on to individual plates. Sprinkle with the parsley and serve immediately.

A vibrantly colourful pasta dish. The addition of eggs and cream to the saffron makes it wonderfully rich and tasty – perfect for lunch on sunny, summer days.

pasta with saffron
pasta allo zafferano

serves 4

1 sachet of saffron powder or a large pinch of saffron strands

400 g (14 oz) spaghetti or tagliatelle

250 ml (9 fl oz) single cream

100 g (3½ oz) Parma ham, finely chopped

50 g (2 oz) freshly grated Parmigiano Reggiano

2 egg yolks, beaten

a large pinch of paprika or cayenne pepper

2 tbsp chopped fresh flat leaf parsley

sea salt

method

First, prepare the saffron. If you are using a sachet of saffron powder, dissolve it in 2 tablespoons of boiling water. If you are using saffron strands, infuse them in a little hot water for 30 minutes.

Bring a large pan of salted water to a rolling boil. Throw in the pasta and stir, cover and return the pan to the boil then remove the lid and cook until al dente.

Meanwhile, heat the cream to boiling point then take off the heat and stir in the ham, Parmigiano Reggiano and saffron liquid. Whisk in the beaten egg yolks.

Drain the pasta thoroughly then return it to the cooking pan and pour over the saffron sauce.

Mix together thoroughly, then add the paprika or cayenne and stir through.

Transfer to a warmed serving dish, sprinkle with the parsley, and serve.

I like the idea of being able to eat delicious pasta in an informal outdoor setting, even at a barbecue. This pasta dish can be cooked as usual but then finished off on a barbecue. Make sure the foil or baking parchment used to wrap the spaghetti is secure so you avoid spillage or overcooking. If you do use a barbecue to finish the dish, take care that the heat is very gentle.

spaghetti parcels
spaghetti al cartoccio

serves 4

400 g (14 oz) spaghetti
extra virgin olive oil
8 ripe tomatoes, skinned and
coarsely chopped
2 garlic cloves, finely chopped
¼ tsp chopped dried chilli
4 tbsp chopped fresh flat leaf parsley
about 12 cooked, peeled tiger prawns
sea salt and freshly ground
black pepper

method

Cook the spaghetti until only just al dente: if anything, it needs to be slightly undercooked. Drain, cool and rinse the pasta in cold water then coat it lightly in olive oil to prevent sticking. Set aside, or if taking on a barbecue picnic, pack it in a sealed box.

Put the tomatoes in a bowl and add the garlic, chilli and parsley. Stir together and season to taste, then add enough olive oil to just cover the surface of the tomato sauce. Mix together thoroughly then add the prawns and stir again.

Leave the sauce to stand for at least 2 hours or overnight. If taking on a barbecue picnic, make sure you pack the sauce securely in a sealed box.

Preheat the oven to 200ºC (400ºF) Gas 6 or heat a barbecue to a gentle heat.

For each serving of pasta, take 2 large squares of baking parchment or foil, place one on top of the other and put equal piles of spaghetti in the centre of each pair, so that you have 4 separate piles.

Divide the tomato mixture between each mound of spaghetti and then wrap the parcels up securely, making sure there are no gaps where the juices could seep out.

Place the parcels on a baking sheet and either place in the oven for about 10 minutes, or put on to the barbecue for about 12 minutes. The spaghetti needs to heat through, rather than cook.

Place each hot spaghetti parcel on a plate and serve, leaving everyone to unwrap their own parcels at the table and enjoy the fragrant steam that emerges from the pasta.

This dish is fantastically easy and it's always a winner. The perfect recipe for those summer days when it is too hot to be very innovative – or to spend too long at the stove! I have chosen tagliatelle because they cook so quickly.

tagliatelle with pancetta and mushrooms
tagliatelle con pancetta e funghi

serves 4

75 g (3 oz) pancetta, cubed
1 tbsp extra virgin olive oil
1 carrot, finely chopped
1 celery stick, finely chopped
1 onion, finely chopped
200 g (7 oz) fresh mushrooms,
thinly sliced
400 g (14 oz) fresh tagliatelle
2 tbsp fresh flat leaf parsley, chopped
sea salt and freshly ground
black pepper
freshly grated Parmigiano Reggiano,
to serve

method

Fry the pancetta in the oil with the carrot, celery and onion for about 5 minutes, then add the mushrooms and cook gently until softened.

Meanwhile, bring a large pot of salted water to the boil and cook the tagliatelle until it is al dente. Drain, return the pasta to the hot pan and dress with the pancetta and mushroom sauce.

Toss together, adding the parsley and black pepper. Serve at once with the cheese.

This Italian picnic dish could not be further from the usual pies and sandwiches eaten on an English picnic. But it is the kind of dish my Italian friends and I would normally prepare outdoors, complete with wood fire and a huge pot of pasta! Ah, what memories…

penne and potatoes with sausages and onions
penne e patate con le salsicce e cipolle

serves 4

1 large potato, peeled and thickly sliced

400 g (14 oz) penne

3 tbsp extra virgin olive oil

1 large onion, chopped

2 large Italian sausages, skinned

1 wine glass dry white wine

100 g (3½ oz) freshly grated pecorino cheese

sea salt and freshly ground black pepper

method

Put the potato slices in a large pot containing enough water to cook the pasta as well. Add salt and boil until the potato is about half cooked. Add the pasta and continue to boil until the pasta is al dente.

Meanwhile, heat the oil in a separate pan and fry the onion until soft.

Grill or barbecue the sausages until cooked through, then crumble the cooked meat into the pan with the onions. Add the wine and raise the heat to evaporate the alcohol then remove from the heat.

Drain the potatoes and pasta, return them to the cooking pot and add the onion and sausage mixture along with half the pecorino cheese.

Mix everything together, season to taste, then transfer into a serving dish. Sprinkle with the remaining cheese and serve at once.

This is a special looking first, or main, course which is actually very simple to prepare, although the recipe looks a bit lengthy. I like to use red peppers but yellow ones also look and taste delicious. It is important that the pasta is small enough to sit comfortably amongst all the other ingredients.

pasta timbales with roasted peppers
timballini di pasta con i peperoni arrostiti

serves 4

extra virgin olive oil

1 onion, chopped

1 x 200 g can chopped tomatoes

a handful of fresh basil leaves

200 g (7 oz) fresh pennette pasta

1 mozzarella, cubed

freshly grated Parmigiano Reggiano, to taste

lemon meatballs (*see recipe on page 33*)

4 large red peppers

sea salt and freshly ground black pepper

method

Preheat the oven to 180°C (350°F) Gas 4.

Heat 2 tablespoons of olive oil in a pan and fry the onion until soft but not coloured. Add the tomatoes and stir. Simmer for 10 minutes, then add the basil and seasoning.

Meanwhile, heat a large pan of salted water and boil the pasta until al dente. Drain, return the pasta to the pan and lightly coat with olive oil. Pour in the sauce and toss to thoroughly combine the sauce and pasta. Add the mozzarella, Parmigiano Reggiano (to taste) and the cooked meatballs.

Heat the grill and turn the peppers over or under the heat until soft and blackened all over. Keep the peppers on a tray under an overturned bowl to steam until cool enough to handle. Skin and deseed the peppers and cut them into large slices. Use the peppers to line 4 oiled dariole moulds or soufflé dishes. Pack with the pasta then fold the peppers back over the top to encase the filling.

Place the moulds on a baking sheet and bake in the oven for about 10 minutes. Remove from the oven and leave to rest for 5 minutes then turn out on to individual serving plates. Serve with a wild rocket salad, lightly dressed with oil and lemon juice.

A very quick and deliciously fresh-tasting recipe. You can vary the flavour slightly by using mint or parsley instead of basil. This will also work with Mascarpone, but if you use this the end result will be much richer and more creamy.

pasta with ricotta and lemon zest
pasta con ricotta e limone

serves 6

350 g (12 oz) fresh ricotta
grated zest of 1¹/₂ large lemons
a large handful of fresh basil leaves
4 tbsp freshly grated Parmigiano Reggiano
450 g (1 lb) short pasta, such as conchiglie, penne or farfalle
sea salt and freshly ground black pepper

TO GARNISH
fresh basil leaves
grated lemon zest
freshly grated Parmigiano Reggiano
extra virgin olive oil

method

First, put the ricotta, lemon zest, basil and Parmigiano Reggiano into a food processor. Whizz for about 2 minutes or until all the ingredients have blended together thoroughly.

Heat a large pan of salted water for the pasta. As soon as the water comes to a rolling boil, take 2–3 tablespoons and add it to the cheese mixture to loosen the texture and make the sauce really smooth. Season the sauce to taste and set aside until required.

Toss the pasta into the pan of boiling water and stir thoroughly. Cook for the required amount of time and drain as soon as it is tender.

Return the pasta to the hot pan, pour over the ricotta sauce and toss everything together very thoroughly. Serve at once in a warmed dish, garnished with fresh basil and grated lemon zest and with extra Parmigiano Reggiano and olive oil offered separately.

This classic Italian summer dish is perfect either hot or cold, and is amazingly easy to prepare. Make sure you use large, round tomatoes, such as beefsteak tomatoes, and they are ripe but firm.

rice-filled baked tomatoes
pomodori al forno ripieni di riso

serves 6

1 large potato
6 large ripe firm tomatoes, such as beefsteak
200 g (7 oz) long-grain rice
2 garlic cloves, finely chopped
75 ml (3 fl oz) extra virgin olive oil
10 fresh basil leaves, torn into shreds
1 tbsp dried oregano
a handful of fresh flat leaf parsley, finely chopped
sea salt and freshly ground black pepper

method

Preheat the oven to 180°C (350°F) Gas 4.

Cut the potato into 6 thick slices about the same circumference as the tomatoes. Slice off the tops from the tomatoes and set them aside. Scoop out the inside of the tomatoes, discard the seeds and chop the flesh and put it into a bowl.

Add the raw rice and the garlic, half the olive oil and all the herbs to the tomatoes and season thoroughly.

Fill the tomatoes with the rice mixture then put the lids back on the tomatoes. Arrange the tomatoes in a roasting tin, wedging them in place with the potatoes. Sprinkle with the remaining oil and drizzle over a little water so that the tomatoes just sit in a little liquid.

Cover the tin loosely with foil and bake in the oven for about 1 hour or until the rice and tomatoes are soft all the way through. Remove the foil for the last 10 minutes of the baking time to allow the tomatoes and potatoes to colour a little. Serve hot or cold.

Crespoline is the Tuscan word for little stuffed crepes or pancakes. The filling is usually based around ricotta. A very traditional recipe is to fill the crespoline with a mixture of ricotta cheese and chopped, cooked spinach, but the asparagus alternative given here is also delicious.

The batter recipe makes 12 pancakes but as you only need 4 for this recipe, you can freeze the rest. If you want 12 crespoline, you need to make three times as much filling.

crespoline with ricotta and spinach
crespoline ripiene di ricotta e spinaci

serves 4

FOR THE CRESPOLINE (MAKES 12)
125 g (4 oz) plain white flour
½ tsp salt
2 eggs, thoroughly beaten
300 ml (½ pint) milk, or a mixture of milk and water
a little unsalted butter or sunflower oil, for frying

FOR THE FILLING (MAKES 4 CRESPOLINE)
6–8 tbsp ricotta
5–6 tbsp cooked, chopped spinach or chard
3 tbsp freshly grated Parmigiano Reggiano
grated nutmeg
1 egg, beaten
extra virgin olive oil, for brushing
sea salt and freshly ground black pepper

method

First, make the pancakes by mixing together all the crespoline ingredients, except the butter or oil, to make a smooth, fairly thin batter. Make sure there are no lumps whatsoever!

Heat a frying pan until it is hot then add a small lump of butter or a scant teaspoon of sunflower oil. Pour in a little batter and swirl the pan so that it barely covers the bottom of the pan.

Cook on one side for about 1 minute, then flip the pancake over and cook the other side for 1 minute. Tip out on to a plate to cool.

Make all 12 crespoline in the same way and either use them all (remember, you will need to use three times as much filling) or freeze them for another occasion.

Preheat the oven to 190°C (375°F) Gas 5 and oil an ovenproof dish with olive oil.

For the filling, mash the ricotta until smooth. Mix it with the spinach, half the Parmigiano Reggiano, a little nutmeg, the egg and season.

Divide the filling between 4 of the pancakes and roll them up. Sit them in the oiled dish. Brush with a little more olive oil and sprinkle with the remaining Parmigiano Reggiano.

Bake the pancakes in the oven until heated through and golden brown on top (about 15 minutes). Serve hot.

ALTERNATIVE
• Fill the crespoline with cooked asparagus rolled in Parma ham and covered with a thin layer of light béchamel sauce and thin slices of fontina cheese. Place in the oven until bubbling and lightly browned.

This traditional Piemontese recipe is simple but delicious. It is made with easily available ingredients like onion, butter, stock and Parmigiano Reggiano. Just pile it on to warmed plates, serve and let the comfort eating commence.

risotto with parmigiano reggiano
risotto alla parmigiana

serves 4

3 tbsp unsalted butter

1 onion, finely chopped

350 g (12 oz) arborio rice

1 wine glass dry white wine

up to 2 litres (3½ pints) rich chicken stock, kept hot

5 tbsp freshly grated Parmigiano Reggiano

sea salt and freshly ground black pepper

method

Melt half the butter in a large saucepan and fry the onion gently until very soft but not coloured. Add all the rice and thoroughly toast the grains for about 5 minutes.

Add the wine and stir for 1 minute or until all the alcohol has evaporated. Then add 3 ladlefuls of stock and stir thoroughly. Reduce the heat to low and continue to stir and add the stock 1½ ladlefuls at a time, letting the rice absorb the liquid before adding more stock. Don't rush it!

As soon as the rice is cooked – it should be tender but still slightly firm to the bite – remove from the heat and stir in the Parmigiano Reggiano and the remaining butter. Stir, taste and season as required.

Cover the pan and leave the risotto to rest for about 4 minutes, then stir again and serve on individual plates.

This is a special risotto full of wonderful, aromatic flavours. It deserves to be served with a very special bottle of wine, so make sure you have one waiting in the wings so you can make this dish truly memorable.

roasted pepper, ham and mascarpone risotto
risotto ai peperoni arrosto con pancetta e mascarpone

serves 4

3 large, firm peppers

50 g (2 oz) unsalted butter

1 onion, finely chopped

2 garlic cloves, peeled and crushed

250 g (9 oz) risotto rice

1.5–2 litres ($2^3/_4$–$3^1/_2$ pints) vegetable or chicken stock, kept hot

1 tbsp extra virgin olive oil

60 g ($2^1/_2$ oz) pancetta, cubed

2 tbsp finely chopped fresh flat leaf parsley

5 tbsp mascarpone

75 g (3 oz) freshly grated Parmigiano Reggiano

sea salt and freshly ground black pepper

1 tbsp finely chopped fresh chives, to serve

method

Light the grill and heat to medium.

Grill the peppers all over until the outer skin is blackened then put them immediately on to a chopping board and cover with a bowl. Leave to stand and cool for about 10 minutes.

Holding the peppers under cold running water, gently rub off the charred outer skin using a new scouring pad (the flesh of the skinned peppers will probably be brown in patches). Cut the peppers in half and remove and discard all the inner seeds and membranes. Then cut the peppers into thin strips and set aside.

Melt the butter in a large, heavy-based saucepan and fry the onion gently until soft and transparent. Add the garlic and three-quarters of the peppers. Stir gently over a low heat for about 3 minutes.

Add the rice. Mix with the peppers and onions for about 5 minutes or until the rice grains are coated in the butter and crackling hot.

Add the first ladleful of hot stock and stir until most of the liquid has been absorbed by the grains. Then add another ladleful of stock. Continue in this way until the rice is plump and tenderly swollen.

Meanwhile, heat the olive oil in a separate pan and fry the pancetta until it is brown and crisp.

When the rice is cooked through but slightly al dente, remove the pan from the heat and stir in the seasoning to taste. Add the parsley, the remaining peppers, the mascarpone, cooked pancetta and Parmigiano Reggiano. Stir, then cover and leave to stand for about 3 minutes.

Transfer the risotto to a warmed platter or individual plates and sprinkle with the chopped chives. Offer extra cheese at the table.

Amazingly delicious and perfectly summery! Take your time when both cooking and eating this sensational risotto. You can vary the choice of seafood according to what is available.

seafood risotto
risotto ai frutti di mare

serves 6

450 g (1 lb) vongole (baby clams)
450 g (1 lb) mussels
250 g (9 oz) small, raw prawns
250 g (9 oz) raw langoustines or large prawns
1 bottle (750 ml) dry white wine
150 ml (5 fl oz) extra virgin olive oil
1.2 litres (2 pints) strong fish stock, kept at simmering point

½ dried red chilli pepper, finely chopped
3 garlic cloves, finely chopped
3 tomatoes, skinned, deseeded and coarsely chopped
3 tbsp chopped fresh flat leaf parsley, plus extra for garnishing
500 g (1 lb) carnaroli rice
sea salt and freshly ground black pepper

method

Wash all the seafood thoroughly, taking care to remove any beards or grit as you go.

Pour a glass of the wine into a deep frying pan. Add the vongole and steam until all the shells have opened. Remove any vongole that do not open and discard. When the shellfish are cool enough to handle, remove three-quarters of the vongole from their shells and set them aside along with the ones still in their shells. Strain the juices from the pan through a fine sieve and into the stock.

Cook the mussels in the same way as the vongole. When they are done, put them aside until required and add the juices to the stock.

Heat 3 tablespoons of the olive oil in a separate pan and quickly fry the prawns until bright pink and cooked through. Turn frequently and baste with wine. When they are cool enough to handle, peel and devein the prawns, adding the shells and heads to the simmering fish stock and setting the prawns aside.

Heat a further 3 tablespoons of olive oil and quickly fry the langoustines until cooked through, turning frequently and basting with wine. When they are cooked through, remove from the pan and take off the legs and claws. Cut the body section open with sharp scissors and remove all the flesh, add the carcasses to the stock pot. Set aside the claws, legs and reserved flesh with the peeled prawns.

Now heat the remaining oil in a large pan and fry the chilli, garlic, tomatoes and parsley for 2 minutes. Next, add the rice and stir thoroughly to coat it in the oil and tomatoes. When it is crackling hot, add a glass of wine. Stir while the alcohol evaporates (about 2 minutes).

Begin to add the stock a ladleful at a time. Stir and allow the grains to absorb each addition of stock before adding more liquid.

Alternate additions of wine and hot stock (this will need to be strained into the risotto to remove any debris), until all the wine has been used.

Continue to add the stock until the risotto is about two-thirds cooked, then add the seafood, including the fish still in their shells. Carry on cooking the risotto as before, adding the fish stock gradually and stirring continuously.

When the rice is creamy but still firm to the bite, transfer the risotto on to a warmed platter and arrange it so that most of the claws and shells are on the top. Sprinkle with chopped parsley and serve at once.

3.

salads & vegetables
INSALATA & VERDURA

There is nothing more satisfying than a colourful and delicious salad on a hot summer's day. Here is a selection of different salads and vegetable dishes that use a variety of tasty, original and balanced ingredients.

I adore the flavour of asparagus cooked like this, and the addition of the parsley pesto makes it into a very special summer dish. You can use classic basil pesto if you prefer. For a more colourful salad, add some strips of carrot, sliced with a peeler and chargrilled, or add a few strips of roasted red and yellow pepper. You could also try pistachio nuts instead of the pine kernels to make a nuttier-tasting pesto.

chargrilled asparagus with parsley pesto
asparagi ai ferri con pesto di prezzemolo

serves 4

450 g (1 lb) fresh asparagus, cleaned, trimmed and washed

200 ml (7 fl oz) extra virgin olive oil

a large bunch of fresh flat leaf parsley, stalks removed

3 garlic cloves

2–3 tbsp pine kernels

3 tbsp freshly grated Parmigiano Reggiano

sea salt and freshly ground black pepper

method

Preheat the grill until very hot. Brush the asparagus all over with 3 tbsp of the olive oil and grill on all sides, turning frequently until the asparagus spears are soft all the way through and slightly blackened on the outside.

Meanwhile, make the pesto. Put the parsley and garlic into a food processor and whizz until finely chopped.

Heat a small frying pan and toss in the pine kernels, toasting them quickly until lightly coloured. Add them to the parsley and garlic.

Turn on the food processor and gradually add the remaining oil until you have a smooth, fairly liquid sauce. Add the Parmigiano Reggiano and season to taste.

Pour the pesto into a bowl and place the cooked asparagus on a plate. Just before serving, drizzle the asparagus generously with the pesto and serve at once.

A very simple salad that makes a perfect first course. The balsamic vinegar is an alternative to the more traditional dressing of lemon juice, although if you prefer you could use wine vinegar or even lemon juice. For a more filling salad add a can of drained, flaked tuna.

green bean and egg salad
insalata di fagiolini e uova sode

serves 6

250 g (9 oz) fine green beans
3 hard-boiled eggs
4 spring onions, finely chopped
3 tsp balsamic vinegar
8 tbsp extra virgin olive oil
sea salt and freshly ground
black pepper

method

Drop the beans into a large pan of boiling water and cook until just tender. Drain and rinse them in cold water and then arrange in a salad bowl.

Chop the hard-boiled eggs and scatter over the beans then add the spring onions.

Mix the balsamic vinegar with the oil and season with salt and pepper. Drizzle over the salad and toss everything together before serving.

This fabulously colourful salad combines simple fresh ingredients to give both colour and flavour, making it a true summer classic. Make sure you use only the finest ingredients for the best results. You can buy good-quality black olive paste in most large supermarkets.

tomato, cucumber and onion salad
insalata di pomodori, cetrioli e cipolle

serves 8

6 large tomatoes, peeled and cut into large dice

2 small cucumbers, peeled and cut into large dice

2 large sweet red onions, cut into very small dice

3–4 tbsp coarsely chopped fresh flat leaf parsley,

6 tbsp black olives, chopped

2 tbsp black olive paste

2 tbsp lemon juice

2 tbsp extra virgin olive oil

method

Put all the vegetables into a large bowl and mix them together gently. Mix in the parsley and then add the olives and stir again.

Make the dressing by combining the black olive paste, lemon juice and olive oil. If the mixture is too thick, add a little more olive oil, and mix thoroughly.

Pour the dressing over the salad. The juices from the vegetables should help to loosen the dressing. Mix thoroughly and serve at once with crusty bread.

Remember to dress the potatoes while they are still hot as they will taste much better and will completely absorb all the flavours in the dressing. Use small, sweet new potatoes for the best results, and make sure they are cooked all the way through – no al dente potatoes please!

italian potato salad
insalata di patate

serves 4–6

425 g (15 oz) small new or
salad potatoes
½ red onion, finely chopped
4 tbsp fresh basil leaves, torn
into shreds
12 cherry tomatoes, halved
about 3 handfuls of mixed salad
leaves, to serve

FOR THE DRESSING
5 tbsp extra virgin olive oil
2 tbsp good-quality balsamic vinegar
1 garlic clove, finely minced
sea salt and freshly ground black
pepper to taste

TO GARNISH
25 g (1 oz) freshly grated
Parmigiano Reggiano
fresh basil leaves

method

Cook the potatoes in plenty of lightly salted boiling water until tender – approximately 15–20 minutes. Drain and cut the potatoes in half while they are still hot. Put the potatoes in a large bowl and add the onion, basil and tomatoes.

Quickly shake all the dressing ingredients together in a screw-topped jar until everything is well blended and emulsified. Check the seasoning and adjust as required. (You could do this in a liquidizer if you prefer.)

Pour the dressing over the potatoes and tomatoes while they are still warm so they absorb the flavours. Toss to ensure everything is well coated.

To serve, arrange the salad leaves on a platter and spoon the warm potato salad on top. Sprinkle with the Parmigiano Reggiano and garnish with the basil leaves. Serve at once.

ALTERNATIVES

- Substitute rocket leaves for basil for a more peppery flavour.
- In Calabria they make a potato salad with sliced potatoes, lots of sliced red onions and sliced tomatoes. Great with barbecues!
- For a less garlicky taste, drop the garlic clove into the vinegar and leave to stand for 15 minutes or longer (up to 2 hours) for the flavour to be released into the dressing. Discard the garlic before using the dressing.
- An alternative dressing for potato salad is pesto mixed with a little extra virgin olive oil to loosen the consistency a little. Add a few sun-dried tomatoes, cut into thin strips, for extra texture and sweetness.

You can use shop-bought or freshly made mayonnaise for this recipe, although homemade mayonnaise always tastes so much nicer. In any case, I would recommend that you taste the jar of shop-bought mayonnaise before using it, so that you can adjust the seasoning accordingly.

pasta salad
insalata di pasta

serves 4

300 g (10 oz) penne or other short pasta

2 tsp extra virgin olive oil

250 g (9 oz) good-quality canned tuna fish in olive oil, drained and flaked

2 handfuls black olives, pitted and coarsely chopped

1 large handful of chopped fresh flat leaf parsley

1 tbsp capers, rinsed and finely chopped

2 large red peppers, deseeded and sliced into strips

sea salt and freshly ground black pepper

FOR THE MAYONNAISE

slice of lemon

1 egg

300 ml (½ pint) sunflower oil or half sunflower half extra virgin olive oil

mustard, vinegar, garlic, herbs, to flavour (optional)

method

Bring a large pan of salted water to the boil. Add the pasta and cook until al dente then drain. Rinse thoroughly with cold water and toss in a bowl with the extra virgin olive oil.

Combine all the salad ingredients together, season then serve immediately dressed with mayonnaise or leave to stand for up to 4 hours before dressing and serving.

To make the mayonnaise, first make sure the liquidizer or blender jug is scrupulously clean by wiping the inside with a slice of lemon to remove any trace of grease

Break the egg into the liquidizer or blender jug and then whizz for about 1 minute with the blade attachment.

Whizz for about 1 minute. Slowly begin to drizzle in the oil, keeping the food processor running all the time.

The egg and oil will begin to amalgamate, thickening and turning a creamy, pale yellow. Take care not to over-blend at this point.

When the mayonnaise is firm, add seasonings such as a tablespoon of vinegar or lemon juice, a teaspoon of mustard, a crushed garlic clove or a few tablespoons of chopped herbs to flavour.

I have to confess to not being a fan of either fresh tuna or cold pasta salads, but in this particular recipe it all seems to work rather well! Make sure you use the right shape and size of pasta for the best results. On a picnic, you can take the salad mixed together except for the tuna, which you can cook over the barbecue at the last minute, then add into the salad just before serving.

pasta salad with fresh chargrilled tuna
pasta fredda al tonno fresco

serves 4

400 g (14 oz) pennette

2 thick fresh tuna steaks

3 tbsp extra virgin olive oil

juice of $\frac{1}{2}$ lemon

a large pinch of dried oregano

1 tbsp salted capers

3 large ripe tomatoes, peeled, deseeded and coarsely chopped

2 tbsp chopped fresh flat leaf parsley

sea salt and freshly ground black pepper

method

Bring a large pan of salted water to a rolling boil, throw in the pasta and stir. Cover and return the pan to the boil then uncover and boil until just tender.

Meanwhile, grill or barbecue the tuna steak until just cooked through, but pink in the middle. Set aside to cool.

Drain then rinse the pasta in cold water until completely cold. Drain thoroughly again and transfer to a large bowl.

Pour over the olive oil and mix together with your fingers to coat all of the pasta and separate the pieces.

Cut the fish into cubes or strips and mix thoroughly with the lemon juice, oregano and capers. Finally, stir in the tomatoes and season to taste.

Add the tuna mixture to the oiled pasta and mix together thoroughly. Then add the parsley and mix again.

Season with more pepper and salt, if required.

Transfer to a serving platter and chill until required. Allow the dish to return to room temperature before serving.

A speedy salad that's ideal for picnics or as a light starter on a hot day. Speck is a smoked, cured ham, which comes from north-eastern Italy. You can also use prosciutto crudo if you prefer, although the smoky flavour of the speck does add more interest to the dish.

baby mozzarella salad with speck and rocket
insalata di mozzarelline con speck e rucola

serves 4

24 baby mozzarella balls, or large
mozzarella, cut into 24
walnut-sized cubes
24 thin slices speck
100 g (3$^1/_2$ oz) fresh rocket
extra virgin olive oil
freshly ground black pepper

method

Wrap each ball of mozzarella in a slice of speck, securing it with a wooden cocktail stick.

Put the wrapped mozzarella in a shallow salad bowl. Scatter over the rocket leaves then dress liberally to taste with olive oil and a little pepper.

It is always best to buy your bresaola sliced from a whole piece of meat rather than in a packet because then you know it is fresh and you can make sure it is cut as you want it. The secret with cured meats is always to try and eat them as soon as possible after slicing, so buy the meat on the day you make the salad if you can.

bresaola with rocket
bresaola con la rucola

serves 4

200 g (7 oz) bresaola, thinly sliced
2 large handfuls of rocket
4 tbsp extra virgin olive oil
2 tbsp balsamic vinegar
sea salt and freshly ground
black pepper

method

Arrange the bresaola on a platter then scatter over the rocket leaves. Whisk together the oil, balsamic vinegar and seasoning, then drizzle over the finished dish. Serve at once.

A real classic for any Italian summer! For the best presentation and taste, make sure the vegetables are cut evenly. Remember to dress the vegetables and the rice while they are still warm so they absorb the flavours from the other ingredients. This is a great salad for picnics and barbecues – or in fact for any outside eating and parties. You can vary the ingredients according to your personal taste.

classic italian rice salad
insalata di riso

serves 4

250 g (9 oz) long-grain rice
1 medium potato, chopped
1 carrot, roughly chopped
50 g (2 oz) French beans,
roughly chopped
1 small courgette, roughly chopped
2 hard-boiled eggs, finely chopped
4 anchovy fillets, chopped (optional)
1 tbsp capers, rinsed and
coarsely chopped
1 tbsp chopped fresh flat leaf parsley

FOR THE DRESSING
6 tbsp extra virgin olive oil
2 tsp lemon juice
sea salt and freshly ground
black pepper

method

Boil the rice in lightly salted water for around 18 minutes, or until tender. Drain the rice thoroughly and set aside in a large bowl.

Meanwhile, boil the potato for 5–10 minutes, then add the carrot and cook for a further 5 minutes, then add the beans and courgette and cook until all the vegetables are tender but not soft. Drain thoroughly then cut into even dice.

Add the eggs, anchovies (if using), capers, parsley and vegetables to the warm rice and mix thoroughly. Use a very large spoon or your hands to distribute everything evenly.

Combine the olive oil and lemon juice, then pour the dressing over the rice. Mix again and season to taste. Leave to stand for at least 1 hour before serving so the flavours have time to develop. If you need to chill the salad, always make sure you bring it back to room temperature before serving.

Serve on a bed of lettuce leaves or use as a filling for beef tomatoes. Alternatively, just serve straight from a pretty serving bowl.

These individual rice salads are made in small moulds lined with prosciutto. You can, of course, use any kind of moulds you like, even plastic cups at a pinch, or make one large mould. If speck is hard to come by, use prosciutto crudo (unsmoked cured ham) instead.

rice salad moulds with prosciutto
insalatine di riso con prosciutto

serves 4

100 g (3½ oz) long-grain rice
a little oil, for brushing
200 g (7 oz) thinly sliced
prosciutto
2 red peppers
2 courgettes
1 large carrot
1 celery stick
1 tbsp capers, rinsed
100 g (3½ oz) pitted green or
black olives
a small bunch of fresh basil leaves
extra virgin olive oil, for dressing
and brushing
sea salt and freshly ground
black pepper

method

Boil the rice in salted water until just tender. Drain, rinse and set aside in a large bowl.

Lightly oil 4 ring moulds and line with the prosciutto, allowing the ham to flop generously over the sides.

Blanch the peppers in boiling salted water for about 3 minutes. Drain and rinse then halve and deseed. Cut the flesh into evenly sized small cubes.

Blanch the courgettes in boiling salted water for 5 minutes then drain, rinse and dice the same size as the peppers. Peel and grate the carrot and thinly slice the celery.

Mix the rice with the peppers, courgettes, carrot, celery, capers and olives. Tear the basil leaves into shreds and add them to the salad. Drizzle over some olive oil and season to taste.

Divide this mixture evenly between the four moulds, pressing it down firmly to force out any air. Fold the ends of the prosciutto slices back over the top of the filled moulds.

Refrigerate until required, then carefully slide the rice moulds out on to individual plates, garnishing with any remaining salad before serving.

Any variety of beans will work for this salad: cannellini, lima or borlotti – just use whatever is available. You can use either dried or prepared beans depending on your preference and how much time you have. Fresh borlotti beans bought in their pods should be treated in exactly the same way as dried beans but will need less cooking time.

bean salad
insalata di fagioli

serves 6

300 g (10 oz) canned, fresh or cooked dried beans
2 tbsp chopped fresh flat leaf parsley
5 tbsp extra virgin olive oil
1 tbsp white or red wine vinegar
sea salt and freshly ground black pepper

method

If using dried beans, soak them overnight in cold water, then drain. Boil them quickly for 5 minutes in unsalted water. Drain and rinse, then boil slowly in fresh water until tender. Do not add salt to the water until the beans are tender, otherwise the skins will toughen.

Drain the beans carefully and give them a rinse in cold water. Tip them into a serving bowl and add the parsley. Mix together thoroughly then dress with the olive oil and vinegar, and season with the salt and pepper.

Let the salad stand for about 30 minutes to let the flavours develop, then serve with plenty of crusty bread to mop up the juices.

ALTERNATIVES

• You could add chopped olives, balsamic vinegar, rinsed and chopped capers, finely chopped lemon peel or a mixture of herbs to vary the flavour of this substantial salad.

A deliciously simple way of serving these wonderful, pale beans. Use ripe, juicy tomatoes and large prawns for the best result. For extra flavour and heat add a dried chilli to the garlic at the start of the cooking.

cannellini beans with rosemary and prawns
gamberi e fagioli cannellini al rosmarino

serves 4

200 g (7 oz) ripe tomatoes

6 tbsp extra virgin olive oil

5–6 garlic cloves, finely sliced

1 medium fresh rosemary sprig, leaves removed and chopped

450 g (1 lb) canned or cooked dried cannellini beans

450 g (1 lb) raw shelled giant prawns

sea salt and freshly ground black pepper

TO GARNISH

cooked unshelled prawns

fresh rosemary sprigs

method

Blanch the tomatoes in boiling water for 1 minute then drain, skin and coarsely chop.

Heat half the oil in a wide, shallow pan and fry the garlic and rosemary for 3 minutes. Then add the tomatoes and beans and stir together for a further 5 minutes.

Add the prawns and cook for a further 4 minutes. Season to taste and remove the pan from the heat.

Serve on a platter either hot or cold, drizzled with the remaining oil and garnished with the cooked whole prawns and a few sprigs of fresh rosemary

The pretty pink colour of this salad makes it look unusual, but really appetizing. It also happens to taste very good and makes an unusual addition to any cold buffet or picnic. You can substitute the chives with finely chopped flat leaf parsley instead.

prawn and beetroot rice salad
insalata di gamberetti e rape rosse

serves 4

300 g (10 oz) long-grain rice
1 large boiled beetroot, peeled and diced
200 g (7 oz) cooked peeled prawns
2 spring onions, finely chopped
juice of ½ lemon
5–6 tbsp extra virgin olive oil
sea salt and freshly ground black pepper
2 tbsp finely chopped fresh chives, to garnish

method

First, cook the rice in lightly salted boiling water for about 18 minutes or until tender. Drain, then rinse briefly under cold running water to stop it from cooking any further (only cool it a little as warm rice will absorb the other flavours better). Transfer to a serving bowl.

Add the beetroot and prawns and mix together thoroughly. Add the spring onions, lemon juice and olive oil. Mix again and season to taste with the salt and pepper. Serve at once garnished with the chives.

A great dish for a summer brunch, especially when served with a jug of Bellini (iced Prosecco and fresh white peach juice). Very pretty, luxurious and absolutely delicious.

leeks and pancetta with poached eggs
uova in camicia con la pancetta e i porri

serves 4

200 g (7 oz) leeks, coarsely chopped

1 tbsp unsalted butter

1 tbsp extra virgin olive oil, plus extra
for drizzling

4 thick slices coarse crusty bread

60 g (2½ oz) thinly sliced pancetta

50 ml (2 fl oz) double cream

4 eggs

sea salt and freshly ground
black pepper

2–3 tbsp chopped fresh herbs,
to garnish

method

Cook the leeks slowly in the butter and oil. Season lightly and leave to stew until very soft.

Meanwhile, toast the bread under the grill and fry the pancetta in a non-stick pan until crisp.

Add the cream to the soft leeks and whizz in the food processor until you have a smooth sauce.

Poach the eggs in boiling salted water. Spoon some of the hot leek sauce on to each of the 4 plates, sit a slice of toasted crusty bread on top, drizzle with a little olive oil, then add the poached egg and finally the pancetta. Serve at once, sprinkled with a scattering of chopped fresh herbs.

Courgette flowers are a central ingredient in Italian summer cooking so I could not possibly write this book – inspired as it is by the warmth of the sun on my back – without including a recipe dedicated to these delectable blossoms. The pistil inside the flowers can be bitter, so be sure to remove it (without tearing the flowers) before you begin.

stuffed courgette flowers
fiori di zucchine ripieni

serves 4

2 tbsp extra virgin olive oil

1 large garlic clove, sliced

$^1/_2$ tsp paprika

1 tsp fresh thyme leaves

2 tbsp chopped fresh flat leaf parsley

100 g (3$^1/_2$ oz) couscous

1.5 litres (2$^3/_4$ pints) hot
vegetable stock

150 g (5 oz) finely minced cooked veal,
pork or chicken

12 courgette blossoms,
pistils removed

oil, for deep-frying

40 g (1$^1/_2$ oz) cornflour

40 g (1$^1/_2$ oz) plain flour

500 ml (17 fl oz) sparkling mineral
water, ice cold

sea salt

1 lemon, to serve

method

Heat the oil in a large pan and fry the garlic with the paprika for
4 minutes, then add the herbs and the couscous.

Mix together thoroughly then add the hot stock. Leave the couscous
to swell (about 5 minutes).

When the couscous is plump and swollen, fork it through to separate
the grains then add the meat. Season with salt and stir again. Fill
the flowers with the couscous mixture and set them aside until
you are ready to fry them.

Heat the oil in a large pan suitable for deep-frying and prepare some
kitchen paper to drain the cooked flowers.

Next, make the batter by stirring together the flours and adding a
pinch of salt. Add enough sparkling water to make a smooth paste.

Dip the filled flowers in the batter to coat them completely, then fry
in the hot oil for about 3–4 minutes each, or until crisp and golden
brown. Drain on kitchen paper.

Arrange on a dish with the lemon cut into wedges and serve at once.

In this recipe, the courgettes are stuffed with a meat filling flavoured with Parmigiano Reggiano and nutmeg. Delicious both hot or cold, they are the perfect meal for al fresco eating. The filling also makes delicious meatballs or a meatloaf.

stuffed courgettes
zucchine ripiene

serves 6

12 medium courgettes

300 g (10 oz) minced veal, beef or pork

2 eggs

125 g (4 oz) freshly grated Parmigiano Reggiano

2–3 tbsp chopped fresh flat leaf parsley

4 tbsp fresh breadcrumbs

a pinch of nutmeg

2 tbsp extra virgin olive oil

125 g (4 oz) unsalted butter

3 onions, finely chopped

1 kg (2¼ lb) canned tomatoes, coarsely chopped

sea salt and freshly ground black pepper

method

Boil the courgettes whole in salted water for about 10 minutes or until they are tender but not mushy. Drain and cool.

Meanwhile, mix the meat with the eggs, Parmigiano Reggiano, parsley and breadcrumbs. Season with salt, pepper and nutmeg and stir thoroughly. Heat the olive oil in a large frying pan and lightly brown the mixture.

Core the courgettes using an apple corer or slice in half horizontally and scoop out the central seed core. Chop the flesh removed with the corer. Add this to the meat mixture and stir. Stuff the courgettes with the filling mixture and set aside.

Melt the butter in a pan and fry the onions over a gentle heat until transparent. Add the tomatoes and season to taste. Cover and simmer for about 20 minutes.

When the sauce is cooked, slide in the stuffed courgettes. Cover the pan and simmer the courgettes in the sauce for 20 minutes or until they are cooked right the way through. Make sure the pan is wide and deep enough so that the courgettes are submerged. Serve hot or cold.

This is a very simple dish and a really tasty way to cook green peppers. In Italian cuisine, green peppers are only usually used sliced in salads, if at all! Stuffed peppers are delicious on their own or as an accompaniment to grilled fish (see page 127) or meat.

stuffed peppers
peperoni imbottiti

serves 4

4 very large or 8 small green peppers

300 g (10 oz) stale bread, crusts removed

550 g (1¼ lb) canned tomatoes, deseeded

1 tbsp capers (preferably salted), rinsed and chopped

50g (2 oz) green olives, pitted and sliced

a handful of fresh flat leaf parsley, chopped

2 salted or 4 canned anchovies, filleted and chopped

75 g (3 oz) pecorino cheese, grated

100 ml (3½ fl oz) extra virgin olive oil

sea salt and freshly ground black pepper

method

Preheat the oven to 150°C (300°F) Gas 2.

Keeping the peppers whole, deseed them by cutting a circle around the stems and pulling out the core. Then carefully scoop out the seeds and membranes from inside each pepper.

In a large bowl, soften the bread with a little water. Roughly chop 3 of the tomatoes and add them to the bread with the capers, olives, seasoning, parsley, anchovies, cheese and about 3 tablespoons of the oil. Mix together very thoroughly then spoon the mixture inside the peppers.

Pour the remaining oil into an ovenproof dish and scatter over the remaining tomatoes. Put the peppers in the dish in an upright position and bake for 1 hour, basting frequently with the tomato and oil sauce. Serve hot or cold.

A very rich and filling aubergine dish, in which the aubergines are first fried, then stuffed and baked. It's substantial enough to serve as a main course for three people if you serve a whole aubergine per person, or as a starter for six people if you serve half an aubergine per person.

stuffed fried aubergines
melanzane a scarpone

serves 3–6

3 medium aubergines, sliced in
half lengthways

6 tsp salt

600 ml (1 pint) sunflower oil or light
olive oil, for frying

2 tbsp chopped fresh flat leaf parsley

20 fresh basil leaves, torn into shreds

2 egg yolks, plus 1 egg white

4 tbsp freshly grated Parmigiano
Reggiano

200 g (7 oz) mozzarella, very
finely cubed

50 g (2 oz) Parma ham, finely chopped

sea salt and freshly ground
black pepper

method

Preheat the oven to 160°C (325°F) Gas 3 and oil an ovenproof dish.

Coat the cut side of the aubergines finely with salt and place them upside down in a colander, cover with a weighted plate or lid for about 20 minutes so the bitter juices can drain away. Wash and dry the aubergines.

Cut out the fleshy centre from each aubergine to make a hollow and reserve, discarding any seeds.

Heat the oil until hot and a small piece of bread sizzles instantly. Fry the aubergine boats on both sides for about 4 minutes. Drain very thoroughly on kitchen paper then lay the aubergines in the oiled dish side by side.

Fry the aubergine flesh in the oil until soft. Drain very thoroughly on kitchen paper, then chop very finely. Mix with the parsley, half the basil, the egg and egg white and the Parmigiano Reggiano. Season to taste with salt and pepper.

Mix the remaining basil with the mozzarella and the chopped ham.

Line the aubergine boats with equal quantities of the mozzarella mixture, then cover with the egg mixture.

Bake in the oven for 20–35 minutes, basting occasionally with a little water. Serve at once, hot or cold but not chilled.

This dish is delightfully pretty and fabulously quick and easy to make: the perfect combination for summer cooking and eating. For the best presentation, use a really sharp knife so you can slice the terrine neatly.

pepper and mozzarella terrine
terrina di peperoni e mozzarella

serves 4

3 leeks
2 red peppers
2 yellow peppers
300 g (10 oz) green beans
4 tbsp extra virgin olive oil
5 eggs, beaten
2 tbsp freshly grated Parmigiano Reggiano
400 g (14 oz) buffalo mozzarella, cubed
sea salt and freshly ground black pepper

method

Preheat the oven to 180°C (350°F) Gas 4 and line a 450 g (1 lb) loaf tin with foil.

Remove the tough green tops from the leeks and trim the roots. Cut them in half lengthways. Strip off the larger, wider leaves and blanch them in boiling salted water for 1 minute, then drain and drop them into cold water. Thinly slice the rest of the leeks and set aside.

Roast the peppers in the oven, on the barbecue or under the grill until blackened, then cool and skin, removing the membranes and all the seeds. Cut the peppers into neat strips.

Boil the beans in salted water for about 8 minutes, then drain and refresh in cold water.

Heat the oil in a pan and gently sauté the finely sliced leeks and the green beans for about 5 minutes.

Season the beaten eggs and add the Parmigiano Reggiano to them.

Line the tin with the blanched leek leaves, laying them lengthways and widthways in the tin and allowing them to flop over the sides.

Fill the terrine, starting with a layer of peppers. Next add layers of beaten egg, mozzarella, green beans and leeks. Continue to layer the ingredients in this order until they are all used or the terrine is full.

Wrap the leek leaves over the top of the filled terrine and press down gently. Cover loosely with foil and bake in the oven for 20 minutes. Remove the foil and allow the terrine to finish cooking, uncovered, for a further 15 minutes or so.

Cool for at least 20 minutes (it is especially delicious when served at room temperature) then slice and serve.

This dish is made with lovely, peppery Italian sausages. You could chargrill them on the barbecue and then add them into the other ingredients. This is a camp-fire favourite, perfect for eating outdoors in cold weather.

bean stew with sausages
salsicce e fagioli

serves 6

450 g (1 lb) fresh or dried borlotti
beans soaked overnight in cold water
2 garlic cloves, chopped
1 onion, chopped
1 celery stick, chopped
1 carrot, chopped
2 tsp chopped fresh flat leaf parsley
2 tbsp extra virgin olive oil
1 tbsp tomato purée diluted in
4 tbsp warm water
12 raw Italian sausages
sea salt and freshly ground
black pepper

method

Rinse the soaked beans and cover them with fresh water. Bring to the boil and boil rapidly for 5 minutes. Drain and rinse, then return them to the pan and cover generously with fresh water. Bring back to the boil then simmer slowly for about 45 minutes or until tender.

Fry the garlic, onion, celery, carrot and parsley in the oil until all the vegetables are soft, then add the diluted tomato purée. Mix together thoroughly, then add the sausages.

Fry the sausages for a few minutes until they are sealed and lightly browned then add the beans and all their cooking liquid. Season with salt and pepper then cover.

Simmer the stew for about 30 minutes or until the sauce is rich and thick. Serve warm.

A lovely dish to look at and an even more delicious one to eat, this summer vegetable pie is incredibly easy to make and very transportable too, making it ideal for picnics. You can of course add other vegetables if you wish.

summer vegetable pie
tortino dell'orto

serves 6

1 large aubergine

1 large yellow or red pepper, deseeded

6 tbsp extra virgin olive oil

1 garlic clove

2 eggs

300 g (10 oz) ricotta

40 g (1½ oz) Pecorino cheese, grated

2 tbsp dried breadcrumbs

8 fresh basil leaves, chopped

4 fresh mint leaves, chopped

a small bunch of fresh flat leaf parsley, chopped

3 tbsp milk

sea salt and freshly ground black pepper

method

Preheat the oven to 180°C (350°F) Gas 4. Oil and line a 20 cm (8 inch) flan case.

Cut the aubergine and pepper into small cubes.

Heat 4 tablespoons of the oil in a large pan and fry the garlic until it is golden brown. Scoop out the garlic and discard.

Add the vegetables and fry them for about 5 minutes, stirring continuously. Then lower the heat, cover the pan and leave the vegetables to sweat for about 10 minutes, stirring occasionally.

Meanwhile, beat the eggs with the ricotta, Pecorino, breadcrumbs and herbs. Add the cooked vegetables and milk then stir to mix together thoroughly. Season with the salt and pepper.

Turn the mixture into the flan case and smooth the surface. Drizzle with the remaining olive oil and bake for 35–40 minutes. Serve warm or cold.

As always, when using seafood make sure it is very fresh. The best way to ensure this is to buy it from a good fishmonger, but otherwise, make sure the fish does not smell of anything, and that it looks shiny and fresh as opposed to dull and tired. Fresh fish and shellfish should only ever smell of the clean sea.

warm seafood salad
insalata di mare tiepida

serves 4

1 kg (2¼ lb) fresh mussels, thoroughly scrubbed and beards removed

1 kg (2¼ lb) fresh baby clams (vongole), scrubbed

1 bay leaf

1 lemon, halved

200 g (7 oz) fresh squid, cleaned and cut into neat strips or rings

175 g (6 oz) small raw prawns

4 large raw Mediterranean prawns

6 tbsp extra virgin olive oil

3 tbsp chopped fresh flat leaf parsley

sea salt and freshly ground black pepper

TO SERVE

salad leaves

lemon slices

method

The night before you plan to make the salad, soak the mussels and clams in a bucket of cold water with the bay leaf and one half of the lemon.

To make the salad, begin by boiling the squid in salted water for 25–30 minutes, or until tender.

Drain the mussels and clams then put in a large pan with a little water and steam for about 8 minutes. When all the shells have opened, drain and discard any that remain closed.

Wash all the prawns carefully, put them in a saucepan and cover with cold water. Bring to the boil then cook for 1 minute. Drain and allow the prawns to cool before removing the shells.

Remove the mussels from their shells and put them in a warm bowl with the prawns and squid.

Mix the shellfish together then squeeze over the juice from the remaining lemon half. Add the oil and parsley. Season with pepper to taste, mix again then season with salt.

Serve lukewarm, piled on to the salad leaves and garnished with lemon slices.

A light, colourful and satisfying stew of peppers and chicken perfumed by thyme and spiced up with a little cumin. Serve with boiled rice or a simple risotto with Parmigiano Reggiano for a more substantial dish. Crusty bread is great for mopping up the juices. You can use either turkey, pork or veal, depending on what is available.

summer stew
spezzatino d'estate

serves 4

1 small yellow pepper
1 small red pepper
1 small green pepper
1 small aubergine
625 g (1¼ lb) skinless chicken breasts
3–4 tbsp extra virgin olive oil
1 large shallot, sliced
1 wine glass dry white wine
1 tsp ground cumin
½ tsp cumin seeds, crushed
1 small bunch of fresh thyme leaves
sea salt and freshly ground black pepper

method

Cut the peppers in half, remove the seeds and membranes and cut the flesh into cubes.

Cube the aubergine and place in a colander. Sprinkle over some salt and place a weighted plate on top. Leave for 30 minutes to allow the bitter juices to drain away. Rinse the aubergine and pat dry.

Meanwhile, cut the chicken into cubes. Heat the oil in a large pan and gently fry the shallot until softened. Add the chicken breasts and brown them all over.

Pour the wine into the pan then add all the cumin and thyme. Season to taste and cook for 5–6 minutes then remove the chicken breasts and set them aside.

Add the aubergines and peppers to the pan and stir. Cover the pan and stew the vegetables for about 10 minutes.

Return the chicken to the pan and continue to stew gently, stirring occasionally, until it is thoroughly cooked. Serve hot.

A great combination of colours and flavours for a crunchy salad. This salad is ideal as part of a buffet or as a very light starter. Fennel, as we all know, is very helpful in terms of its digestive qualities, so you could also serve it between one course and another to aid digestion. Please make sure you use really white, crisp, male fennel for the best results. For the record, male fennel is squatter and rounder than the more sinuous female version.

fennel, olive and salami salad
insalata di finocchi, olive e salame

serves 4

2 male fennel heads, thinly sliced
a large handful of black olives, stoned
about 12 slices chilli-flavoured salami,
cut into strips

FOR THE DRESSING
juice of 2 oranges
grated zest of 1 orange
$\frac{1}{2}$ tsp mustard, preferably Italian
Savora
250 ml (9 fl oz) extra virgin olive oil
sea salt and freshly ground
black pepper

method

Mix together the fennel, olives and salami strips and place on a platter or in a bowl.

Combine all the dressing ingredients in a screw-topped jar and shake until all the ingredients are well combined.

Pour the dressing over the salad and toss everything together thoroughly.

Leave to stand for about 30 minutes to allow the flavours to develop, then serve.

4.

hot coals & embers
ALLA GRIGLIA

Recipes for cooking meat, fish, vegetables and
cheese over the grill are all contained in this
chapter. There is even a recipe for polenta and one
for focaccia. As always when using a barbecue,
make sure that you have plenty of hot embers
before you start cooking.

Here are some rough guidelines for successful barbecuing. It is an art with many variables such as size of grill, what kind of fuel is being used (charcoal or wood, or a combination of the two) and how close the grill is to the embers. It is also an art at which you'll become a great deal more efficient and adventurous once you have mastered the basics and with a little practice!

Recommended cooking times for meat

meat	temperature	minutes	
LAMB	high heat	5	for cutlets
		8	for skewers
BEEF STEAKS *2–3 cm (1–1½ ins) thick*	high heat	7	for rare
		10	for medium
		15	for well done
VEAL CHOPS	medium heat	10	
HAMBURGERS	medium heat	7–10	
PORK CHOPS	medium heat	10–15	
CHICKEN PORTIONS	medium to low heat	20	
SAUSAGES	medium to low heat	8–12	

Recommended cooking times for fish

fish	temperature	minutes	
SMALL WHOLE FISH *below 300 g (10 oz)*	high heat	2–3	
LARGE WHOLE FISH *300–350 g (10–12 oz)*	medium heat	6	on each side
SLICES OF FISH *2.5–5 cm (1–2 inches) thick*	medium heat	3	on each side
FILLETS OF FISH *150–200 g (5–7 oz)*	medium to low heat	30	seconds on each side
MOLLUSCS	medium to low heat	10–12	
PRAWNS	low heat	3–4	

The perfect seaside barbecue food! This is a wonderful way to enjoy mussels – especially if they are really fresh. Make the sauce ahead and take it to the beach in a small, screw-topped bottle or jar.

barbecued mussels
cozze alla brace

serves 4

1 kg (2¼ lb) mussels

2–3 lemons, halved

FOR THE SAUCE

a handful of fresh flat leaf parsley, finely chopped

5 tbsp extra virgin olive oil

2 garlic cloves, crushed

grated zest of 1 lemon

sea salt and freshly ground black pepper

method

First, prepare the mussels by scrubbing the shells clean and removing any beards. Wash them thoroughly in several changes of cold water. Heat the grill or barbecue until hot, with plenty of glowing embers in the latter case.

Make the sauce by whisking together the parsley, oil, garlic and lemon zest in a small bowl. As soon as the sauce has emulsified, season to taste and pour into a serving bowl or jar.

Place the mussels on the grill pan and use tongs to move them around. As they begin to open up, squeeze over a few drops of lemon juice. As soon as the mussels are fully open, remove them from the heat.

Quickly put the mussels into a dish. Pour a little of the sauce over each one and eat immediately with your fingers.

This is my favourite way to enjoy these lovely, juicy fruits of the sea. You can cook small lobsters or, even better, fresh crab in the same way.

roasted langoustines
scampi arrosto

serves 4

8 large raw Dublin Bay prawns
6 tbsp extra virgin olive oil
2 garlic cloves, finely chopped
3 tbsp chopped fresh flat leaf parsley
juice of 1 lemon
sea salt and freshly ground
black pepper

method

Preheat the oven to 220°C (425°F) Gas 7 or heat a barbecue until it is hot.

Wash the prawns thoroughly and pat dry. Cut each prawn open on the underside using a pair of sharp scissors and remove the intestinal tube, taking care not to damage the flesh. Put the prawns in a large bowl.

Mix together the remaining ingredients to make a thick sauce. Season to taste, then pour over the prawns. Leave to marinate in the refrigerator for about 30 minutes.

Spread the prawns over a thin metal roasting dish and either place them on the barbecue or roast them in the oven for about 10 minutes, basting frequently with the marinade and turning from time to time. Serve hot or cold.

This is the easiest and simplest way to grill fish on the barbecue. Despite this, I must stress that it is absolutely essential that the fish is as fresh as possible and cut quite thick to avoid it falling apart and cascading into the fire! Grilled fish is especially good when served with Stuffed Peppers (see page 108). You can also bake fish steaks in the oven, wrapped in foil with oil and salt and pepper to preserve flavour and moisture.

grilled fish steaks
pesce ai ferri

serves 4

4 small firm fish steaks such as
swordfish, tuna, cod or salmon
4–5 tbsp extra virgin olive oil or
lemon-flavoured oil
sea salt and freshly ground
black pepper
wedges of lemon, to garnish

method

Heat the grill to medium.

Trim the fish steaks neatly then brush both sides with the oil and season thoroughly with salt and pepper.

Grill the fish steaks for about 4 minutes on each side or until just cooked through. The exact cooking time will depend upon the thickness of the fish.

Serve with a wedge of lemon and stuffed peppers (see page 108).

Fabulous either hot or cold, this dish has a real flavour of Sicily. You can create your own fillings – the possibilities are endless. Just make sure you have threaded the rolls securely on to the sticks so that the end result is as tidy as possible.

stuffed swordfish rolls
involtini di pesce spada

serves 6

1.25 kg (2³/₄ lb) swordfish steaks or 24 steaks, very thinly sliced
4 or 5 slices of stale, crusty bread
2 tbsp extra virgin olive oil
5 tbsp fine dry breadcrumbs

FOR THE CURRANT FILLING
5 tbsp fresh flat leaf parsley leaves
5 garlic cloves
3 tbsp currants, soaked in hot water for 5 minutes and roughly chopped
3 tbsp pine nuts, roughly chopped
1–2 tbsp extra virgin olive oil
sea salt and freshly ground black pepper

FOR THE OLIVE FILLING
4 tbsp pitted green olives
3 tbsp capers
2 tbsp chopped fresh flat leaf parsley
3 tbsp soft white breadcrumbs
4 tbsp grated Caciocavallo, Parmigiano Reggiano or Pecorino cheese
2–3 tbsp extra virgin olive oil
freshly ground black pepper

method

To make the currant filling, chop the parsley and garlic together until very fine. Add the currants and pine nuts, and add salt and pepper to taste. Stir in the olive oil and mix thoroughly.

To make the olive filling, chop the olives, capers and parsley together until fine. Stir in the breadcrumbs and the cheese, moisten with the oil, add seasoning and stir thoroughly.

To prepare the swordfish (if your fishmonger cannot do it for you), first bone and skin the steaks, then cut them into quarters. Slice each quarter into 6 very thin slices so you have 24 slices measuring roughly 7 x 10 cm (3 x 4 inches) and less than 3 mm (¹/₈ inch) thick.

Put 1 teaspoon of one of the fillings on one end of a slice of fish and roll it up as neatly as possible. Continue until all the fish slices and fillings are used.

Thread a piece of bread on to the end of a skewer then a fish roll. Follow with another roll, and carry on until you have 6 skewers, each with 4 rolls of fish and a piece of bread at either end to hold it all in place.

Run a second skewer through the rolls about 2.5 cm (1 inch) distant and parallel to the first, so that they don't spin and break when you turn them.

When all 6 servings are ready, moisten them with the oil and dip them in the breadcrumbs so they are lightly coated. Grill gently, either over barbecue coals or under a grill, for about 8–10 minutes.

The fish rolls can also be cooked in the oven. Preheat the oven to 180°C (350°F) Gas 4, lay the skewers side by side in a lightly oiled baking tray and bake for about 20 minutes, turning once.

A really simple and very easy way to enjoy these two great summer flavours
– fresh salmon and pesto.

grilled salmon steaks with pesto
salmone al pesto alla griglia

serves 4

4 medium-sized fresh salmon steaks
6 tbsp good-quality,
ready-made pesto
3 tbsp extra virgin olive oil
1 tbsp lemon juice
2 tbsp dry white wine
sea salt and freshly ground
black pepper

method

Wipe and trim the salmon steaks and sprinkle with the salt and pepper.

Mix the pesto with the oil, lemon juice and wine then rub the pesto marinade all over the salmon.

Grill or barbecue the salmon on both sides for a total of 10 minutes, spooning over the remaining marinade as the fish cooks.

Serve with boiled new potatoes dressed with extra virgin olive oil and a few ripped leaves of fresh basil.

A very easy and tasty way to enjoy chicken with little effort! You can now buy many different kinds of pesto in jars, made with all kinds of different ingredients. This recipe uses black olive, but you can ring the changes by using other types of pesto, or even make your own version if you prefer. Serve with potatoes that have been roasted in olive oil with garlic and olives.

grilled chicken with black olive pesto
pollo alla griglia con crema di olive nere

serves 4

8 chicken thighs
1 jar ready-made black olive pesto or homemade black olive pâté
1 tbsp finely chopped fresh rosemary leaves
extra virgin olive oil
juice of 1 lemon (optional)
sea salt and freshly ground black pepper

method

Bone the chicken thighs carefully using a pair of sharp scissors and cut away any excess skin, gristle or flesh.

Generously stuff each chicken thigh with the pesto or pâté and wrap the flesh around it to seal.

Close the stuffed thighs using a piece of cook's string or a wooden cocktail stick that has been soaked in cold water. Rub the sealed chicken all over with rosemary, olive oil, salt and pepper.

Grill on a medium heat, sprinkling with the lemon juice (if using), for about 10–15 minutes or until cooked through. Alternatively, sprinkle with the lemon juice and roast in the oven at 190°C (375°F) Gas 5 for approximately 30 minutes or pan-fry in a covered frying pan for 30 minutes or until thoroughly cooked. Serve hot or cold.

A very simple, but delicious dish – the combination of chicken and peppers never disappoints.

chicken and pepper skewers
spiedini di pollo e peperoni

serves 4

2 chicken breasts, cut into 2 cm
(³/₄ inch) cubes
juice of ¹/₂ lemon
3 tbsp extra virgin olive oil
2 tbsp fresh rosemary leaves
1 garlic clove , puréed
4 slices ciabatta, cut into 2 cm
(³/₄ inch) cubes
1 large red onion, cut into thick chunks
2 large yellow or red peppers, cut into
2 cm (³/₄ inch) cubes
sea salt and freshly ground
black pepper

method

Put the chicken cubes in a bowl. Mix together the lemon juice, olive oil, rosemary and garlic. Season with salt and pepper and pour over the chicken. Mix together with your hands until the chicken is thoroughly coated in the marinade. Leave to stand for about 30 minutes.

Meanwhile, soak 4 wooden kebab skewers in water.

To make the skewers, thread on the bread, chicken, onion and peppers until all the ingredients are used up. Start and finish each skewer with a chunk of bread to hold everything together firmly.

Brush the skewers with the rest of the marinade and grill or barbecue for about 10–12 minutes, turning frequently and basting with any remaining marinade or water in order to keep the chicken moist. Serve hot or cold.

These little skewers (spiedini) have an odd name – escaped birds on skewers! Nowadays, I am happy to say, there are far fewer songbirds eaten in Italy! If wild boar sausages are not readily available, use good-quality pork sausages instead.

skewered chicken and boar with sage
spiedino di uccelli scappati

serves 6

12 fresh wild boar sausages
24 very large fresh sage leaves – as big as possible
12 slices bread, cut into 4 x 4 cm (1½ x 1½ inch) squares
3 skinless, boneless chicken breasts, each cut in half
extra virgin olive oil, for brushing
sea salt and freshly ground black pepper

method

Preheat the oven to 190°C (375°F) Gas 5 or heat a barbecue grill until it is medium hot.

Thread the ingredients on to 6 metal or wooden skewers in the following order: sausage, sage leaf, bread, sage leaf, chicken, sage leaf, bread, sage leaf and so on until they are full and all the ingredients are used up.

Brush each skewer lightly with the olive oil and season.

Either roast in the oven, suspended across a baking tray, for about 30 minutes, or cook over a barbecue grill for about 20 to 30 minutes, turning frequently, or until completely cooked through. Serve with extra virgin olive oil drizzled over.

The chicken in this dish becomes completely black on the outside, so it is the flattened shape and black colour which gives it the name of diavola, meaning devil. It is one of those recipes that relies entirely upon the quality of the chicken and the flavours from the wood fire to give its very special flavour.

devil's chicken
pollo alla diavola

serves 6

2 oven-ready chickens, each weighing about 750 g (1 lb 10 oz)

about 6 tbsp extra virgin olive oil

4 tbsp fresh rosemary leaves, coarsely chopped

sea salt and freshly ground black pepper

method

Cut open the chickens along the breastbone and press down hard on the open chickens to flatten them out as much as possible.

Heat the grill or light the barbecue. Rub the chickens all over with the olive oil, salt and pepper. Sprinkle with the rosemary leaves.

Grill them on both sides or until completely cooked through and they are very well browned, if not blackened and thoroughly cooked through but still juicy in the middle. Serve at once, jointed.

This is one of the roast chicken recipes where the stuffing is just as good cold as it is hot, which means you can cook it ahead and serve it cold or transport it to a picnic. You can substitute good-quality thick-cut smoked bacon for the pancetta.

roast chicken with a fennel stuffing
pollo arrosto con ripieno di finocchi

serves 6

1 x 2.5 kg (5lb 8 oz) roasting chicken
about 7 tbsp extra virgin olive oil, plus
extra for roasting
200 g/7 oz smoked pancetta, cubed
1 large onion, chopped
1 large head fennel, finely chopped
1 large potato, cubed
2 garlic cloves, chopped
1 tbsp fresh, chopped rosemary leaves
1 tsp fennel seeds, lightly crushed
150 ml/¼ pint dry white wine
sea salt and freshly ground
black pepper

method

Wipe the chicken then rub the skin and the inside thoroughly with
about 3 tablespoons of the olive oil and seasoning.

To make the stuffing, gently heat about 4 tablespoons of olive oil in a
pan then add the pancetta, onion, fennel, potato, garlic, rosemary
and fennel seeds. Fry for about 5 minutes, stirring frequently.

Pour the wine into the pan and boil off the alcohol for about
1 minute, then simmer gently until all the ingredients are cooked.

Remove the pan from the heat and leave to cool until just tepid.

While the stuffing is cooling, preheat the oven to 200°C (400°F) Gas 6.

Fill the cavity of the chicken with the stuffing, setting aside any
leftovers so they can be cooked in the roasting pan. Close the
chicken with skewers or with cook's string, and place it in an oiled
roasting tin, breast side up.

Slide the chicken into the oven and roast for 25 minutes, then remove
it, turn it over and return to the oven for a further 20 minutes.

Reduce the heat to 180°C (350°F) Gas 4. Turn the chicken once
more then leave to roast for a final 30 minutes. Add any remaining
stuffing to the tin 15 minutes before the end of the roasting time.

To check that the chicken is cooked, pierce the thickest section of the
legs with a metal skewer. If the juices run clear the chicken is
cooked. To check the stuffing and inside of the chicken, push the
skewer deep inside, leave for 10 seconds and then remove it. If the
skewer is not burning hot, leave the chicken to cook a little longer.

Remove the chicken from the oven and leave to rest for 5 minutes
before carving. Serve with the juices and stuffing from the tin.

It really is essential that the liver is cooked over a very high heat so that the meat is just seared. A slow cooking process makes liver rubbery – so avoid it at all costs!

grilled calves' liver and prosciutto
fegato con il prosciutto alla griglia

serves 4

4 large slices calves' liver, trimmed
8 slices Parma ham
dried sage
balsamic vinegar
sea salt and freshly ground
black pepper

method

Carefully wrap each slice of liver in two slices of ham. Make sure the liver is securely encased in the ham by pressing the edges of the ham together firmly. Season with salt and pepper and a very light dusting of dried sage.

Quickly lay on to a preheated barbecue or under a hot grill for about 3 or 4 minutes on either side or until the ham is starting to sizzle and the liver is seared.

Remove the meat from the grill, sprinkle each slice of liver with 2 drops of balsamic vinegar and serve at once.

Bistecca alla Fiorentina is traditionally made using T-bone steaks, but you could make it using ordinary, very thick-cut rump, sirloin or even fillet steak as well. As long as the meat is of a very high quality (preferably organic) it will still taste delicious, even if it's not entirely authentic! The marinating time is quite long, so make sure you start this dish at least a day before you want to eat it.

florentine steak
bistecca alla fiorentina

serves 2

1 x 750 g (1 lb 10 oz) T-bone steak
8 tbsp extra virgin olive oil
4–5 fresh rosemary sprigs
3 garlic cloves, crushed
sea salt and freshly ground
black pepper
2–3 handfuls of wild rocket or 1–2 raw
artichoke hearts, thinly sliced
balsamic vinegar
high quality extra virgin olive oil

method

Put the steak in a shallow dish. Mix together the olive oil, rosemary and garlic and season with salt and pepper. Pour over the steak and leave in the fridge to marinate for 24–48 hours.

Heat a grill or barbecue until it is very hot. Grill the meat to taste (see page 121), turning to cook the steak evenly on both sides.

Scatter with the rocket leaves or artichoke hearts. Drizzle with a little balsamic vinegar and olive oil. Season to taste and serve.

This recipe is made with very rare or raw beef, like carpaccio or steak tartare, so it is essential that very best-quality fresh, tender beef be used. It's a little fiddly to make, but the end result is delicious and really effective.

beef fillet rolls
rotolini di filetto

serves 4

1 large avocado
juice of 1 lime
1 head of celery
1 yellow pepper
400 g (14 oz) fillet of beef, very finely sliced
a bunch of fresh chives
4 tbsp extra virgin olive oil
sea salt and freshly ground black pepper
lettuce leaves, to serve

method

Peel and stone the avocado and mash it in a bowl with half the lime juice and a little salt and pepper.

Separate the celery head into sticks. Cut the paler, tender central sticks into small, thin matchsticks and use the thicker celery for another dish.

Deseed the pepper and cut into matchsticks the same size as the celery.

Place the beef fillet slices on a clean cutting board and spread with the avocado and lime mixture then arrange a few celery and pepper sticks on top.

Roll up each slice of meat, enclosing the avocado, celery and pepper inside. Tie each roll at both ends with a long, strong chive.

Mix together the olive oil with the remaining lime juice to make a dressing and season with salt and pepper.

Either heat a barbecue grill until very hot or heat a dry frying pan over a high heat.

Sear the beef rolls on the barbecue or in the pan for no more than 20 seconds. The meat should be slightly charred all over but not cooked.

Serve on a bed of lettuce doused with the olive oil and lime dressing.

Burgers with an Italian twist! You can add as much garlic as you like, or more chilli if you like the extra heat. I like to omit the ketchup, and instead make a light garlic and herb mayonnaise to serve on the side. If you can't be bothered to make your own mayonnaise, then simply purée a couple of cloves of garlic and mix them thoroughly into ready-made mayonnaise, together with a tablespoon of finely chopped mixed herbs.

italian burgers
hamburger all'italiana

makes 4

550 g (1¼ lb) very lean minced beef steak

1 garlic clove, puréed

a large pinch of dried oregano

12 green olives, stoned and finely chopped

1 tbsp salted capers, rinsed and chopped

a pinch of dried red chillies

a little extra virgin olive oil

sea salt and freshly ground black pepper

TO SERVE

4 slices toasted ciabatta bread

1 garlic clove

extra virgin olive oil

salad leaves

sea salt

lemon juice

method

Break up the meat with your hands then blend in the garlic, oregano, olives, capers and dried chillies. Season with the salt and pepper, then mix again.

Oil your hands and shape the mixture into 4 round, flat burger shapes.

Grill under a high heat or on a barbecue, cooking on both sides until the burgers are cooked to your liking, depending on your personal preference and how thick they are.

Rub the toasted ciabatta with the garlic clove and drizzle over some olive oil. Place the burger on top and serve with a handful of salad leaves dressed with oil, salt and a squeeze of lemon juice.

To make this very fashionable Italian dish, you need to get hold of some really good, tasty and tender beef. There are a variety of sauces that you can serve with the beef to make it even more delicious.

beef tagliata
tagliata di manzo

serves 4–6

1.25 kg (2½ lb) entrecôte steak
5 tbsp extra virgin olive oil
a few fresh rosemary sprigs
3 black peppercorns
3 garlic cloves, sliced
sea salt and freshly ground
black pepper

method

Put the meat in a bowl. Mix together the olive oil, rosemary, peppercorns and garlic. Pour over the meat and stir through thoroughly so it is evenly coated. Leave to marinate for at least 10 minutes.

Meanwhile, heat a wide, dry frying pan until very hot. Lay the marinated meat in the hot pan and sear it on all sides for 8–10 minutes, depending on whether you want it rare, medium or well-done (see page 121). Turn the meat 4 times to avoid it steaming in its own juices, which would make it tough.

At the very end of the cooking time, season with salt and pepper then transfer the meat on to a chopping board, slice and drizzle with the cooking juices.

If serving with one of the sauces on page 146, cover the meat loosely in foil to keep it warm. Cook the sauce in the same pan used to fry the beef so the meat juices add extra flavour.

beef tagliata with capers
tagliata di manzo con i capperi

Put a handful of chopped capers and 2 drained
anchovy fillets into the hot pan and stir
together until the anchovies have all but melted
into the oil. Arrange the meat on a platter, pour
over the sauce and serve.

beef tagliata with salad leaves
tagliata di manzo con le insalate

Shred a small head of radicchio and a large
handful of rocket leaves. Cook quickly in the
hot pan for about 1 minute, stirring until the
leaves have just wilted. Arrange the meat on a
platter. Scatter over the wilted leaves, drizzle
with a little extra virgin olive oil and serve.

beef tagliata with mustard
tagliata di manzo con la senape

Mix together 3 tablespoons of cream and
1 tablespoon of mustard then pour into the hot
pan. Add 1 teaspoon of crushed green or pink
peppercorns. Stir quickly, bringing the cream to
boiling point. Arrange the meat on a platter,
pour over the sauce and serve.

beef tagliata with tomatoes
tagliata di manzo ai pomodori

Blanch 4 tomatoes in boiling water for 1 minute
then drain, skin and roughly chop. Cook the
tomatoes in the hot pan, stirring frequently, for
about 2 minutes. Arrange the meat on a platter.
Pour over the tomatoes, sprinkle with a few
torn basil leaves and serve, drizzled with a little
extra virgin olive oil.

This simple pork and leek mixture is very versatile. I vary its uses by either making it into meatballs (as with this recipe) or flat patties that I cook under a grill or on a barbecue. It can also be baked in the oven to make a tasty meatloaf.

pork and leek patties
polpettine di maiale e porri

serves 4

500 g (1 lb) lean minced pork

2 leeks, 1 large and 1 small

3 tbsp extra virgin olive oil

2 eggs

1 tbsp white wine vinegar

1 tbsp soy sauce

sea salt and freshly ground black pepper

2 tbsp chopped fresh flat leaf parsley, to serve

method

Put the pork in a bowl. Slice the larger of the two leeks very finely and add to the pork.

Trim and slice the small leek lengthways. Gently heat the oil in a large frying pan then add the leek and fry over a low heat until just softened. Season with salt and pepper and keep warm.

Stir the eggs into the pork then add the vinegar and soy sauce. Mix thoroughly to combine all the ingredients then shape into small balls.

Drop the little balls into the frying pan with the cooked leek, turning them gently so that they keep their shape and cook evenly. Cover and leave to simmer gently for about 15 minutes.

Transfer on to a platter, sprinkle with the parsley and serve.

These deliciously simple lamb cutlets are called 'finger burn' in Italian because they must be eaten with your fingers while they are piping hot. You will need to buy tender lamb cutlets and cook them over a high heat to ensure they are cooked through evenly and to perfection! Make sure you use good-quality balsamic vinegar for the best flavour.

barbecued or grilled lamb cutlets
agnello scottadito

serves 4

12 small lamb cutlets
3 garlic cloves, puréed
6 tbsp extra virgin olive oil
3 tbsp very finely chopped fresh
rosemary leaves
sea salt and freshly ground
black pepper
balsamic vinegar

method

Wipe and trim the cutlets, then pierce them in three or four places so that the garlic and rosemary rub can really permeate into the meat.

Mix together the garlic, oil and the rosemary, and beat until thickened and emulsified, seasoning to taste.

Spread the rosemary marinade over the meat and rub it in thoroughly.

Leave to stand for about 10 minutes, then grill quickly until seared on both sides, turning only once. (The cutlets should be charred and blackened on the outside and deliciously juicy and pink on the inside.)

As soon as the cutlets are ready, remove from the heat and drizzle with a few drops of balsamic vinegar and serve at once.

This is a fabulous way to enjoy scallops or oysters. If you can get it, use paper-thin slices of Lardo di Collonnata instead of pancetta. Lardo is cured pork fat. Collonnata is set in the Carrara region, which is famous for its marble. There, the fat is massaged into lengths and rubbed with salt, garlic and herbs. It is then left to cure inside marble containers for about three months before being removed and left to dry on marble slabs. Served in very thin slices, it is white in colour, with a delicately spicy flavour and a distinctively delicate aroma.

barbecued scallops and radicchio
capesante alla brace e radicchio

serves 4

16 large scallops
16 large radicchio leaves
16 paper-thin slices good-quality
pancetta or Lardo di Collonnata
16 tiny fresh rosemary sprigs
2 tbsp extra virgin olive oil or
melted pork fat

method

Wrap each scallop in a radicchio leaf and then in a slice of pancetta or lardo. Secure the wrapping with a wooden cocktail stick and tuck a tiny sprig of rosemary inside each parcel.

Brush lightly with a little olive oil or melted pork fat then lay on a moderate grill or over medium coals and cook until the pancetta or lardo is crisp around the edges, turning two or three times.

I love the taste of radicchio leaves chargrilled over a wood fire. The smoky flavour of the barbecue seems to marry well with the natural bitterness of the leaves. All it then needs is a dressing made with good extra virgin olive oil, a squeeze of lemon juice and a little seasoning to make the perfect accompaniment to grilled meat.

barbecued radicchio
radicchio ai ferri

serves 4

4 large heads of radicchio di Treviso, each with a substantial root stump
extra virgin olive oil
2 lemons, halved
sea salt and freshly ground black pepper

method

Wash the radicchio thoroughly and then slice it cleanly through the centre lengthways. The root stump will hold the leaves together as they cook.

Dry the leaves and then brush all over with olive oil. Lay the radicchio on a hot barbecue and grill quickly on both sides, sprinkling with olive oil and lemon juice to moisten and flavour them.

When softened and charred, sprinkle with salt and pepper and serve.

I like to take the dough on a picnic, well risen and sealed carefully inside a big container to allow it space to continue to rise in the warmth. Great fun can be had slapping the shaped rounds of dough on to the grill once the fire has burned down to an even heat. I promise you this does work, as long as you have oiled the surface of the focaccia thoroughly before attempting to cook it.

barbecue-cooked focaccia
focaccia sulla griglia

makes 6 focaccia

400 g (14 oz) plain strong white flour
25 g (1 oz) fresh yeast
200 ml (7 fl oz) warm water
roughly ground sea salt
2–3 tsp extra virgin olive oil

method

Tip all the flour out on to the worktop.

Mix together the yeast and water then add about 2 tablespoons of the flour. Put this yeast mixture into a lightly floured bowl then place it somewhere warm for about 30 minutes so it can rise.

When it has risen, knead the dough thoroughly. Then add it to the rest of the flour and knead again, adding a little more warm water as needed.

Add some salt and the oil and knead energetically for about 10 minutes.

Transfer this mixture to a large floured bowl and return to the warm place to rise again for about 1 hour or until doubled in size.

When you are ready to make the focaccia, cut the dough into 6 pieces and, with well-oiled hands, shape each piece into a rough round and flatten it between your palms to make a flat bread shape.

Slap each round of dough on to the hot barbecue grill and cook over the hot embers for about 6 minutes, allowing the bread to crisp on one side. Then flip over on to the other side and cook until this is crisp too.

Sprinkle with salt and serve piping hot.

Even plain polenta is delicious sliced and grilled on the barbecue, but it is even better when spiced up with other ingredients, which add flavour and interest. This version of polenta is the perfect foil for salami and other intensely flavoured cured meats and cheeses. It is a great alternative to bread and, once cooled, is very easy to transport, making it ideal for picnics and barbecues. It is seen here with the squid topping from page 16.

green polenta
polenta verde

serves 6–8

About 3 litres (5¼ pints) cold water

450 g (1 lb) tender, leafy broccoli florets

450 g (1 lb) polenta flour

100 g (3½ oz) pancetta, cubed and dry-fried until browned

¼ tsp freshly ground black pepper or crushed chillies

¼ tsp fennel seeds, lightly crushed

sea salt

extra virgin olive oil, for brushing

method

Heat the water in a large pan until it reaches boiling point. Season with 2 pinches of salt, then toss in the broccoli and boil for about 3 minutes.

Gradually trickle the polenta flour into the pan with the broccoli, whisking constantly to avoid any lumps forming. Boil gently for about 30 minutes, stirring constantly with a wooden spoon.

Next, stir in the pancetta and cook for a further 10 minutes.

Season with salt, the pepper or chillies and the fennel seeds. Cook for a further 10 minutes, or until the polenta comes away cleanly from the side of the pan.

Tip out on to a wooden board and leave to cool and solidify.

Once cooled, the polenta can be sliced, brushed lightly with olive oil and grilled on the barbecue or under the grill. Serve crisp and warm with a selection of cured sliced meats and cheeses, or with a topping such as squid – as in the picture.

This is a lovely way to use those delicious mushrooms preserved in oil which you can buy in all good Italian delis. It is very simple to make, unusual in flavour and with just enough acidity to cut the slightly sweet and cloying quality of the aubergines. You could easily substitute preserved peppers for the mushrooms if you prefer.

grilled aubergine with preserved mushroom
melanzane ai ferri con funghi sott'olio

serves 6

2 large aubergines
extra virgin olive oil
1 small tub crème fraîche
1 jar mushrooms preserved in oil, drained
juice of $\frac{1}{2}$ lemon
3 tbsp chopped fresh flat leaf parsley
sea salt and freshly ground black pepper

TO GARNISH
lemon slices
flat leaf parsley sprigs

method

Slice the aubergines thickly lengthways, making sure you have an even number of slices per person. Place the slices in a large colander in layers, sprinkling each layer generously with sea salt. Put a plate on top of the last layer and put a weight on the plate. Put the colander in the sink and leave to drain for about 1 hour so the bitter juices can drain away. Wash and dry all the aubergine slices thoroughly.

Thoroughly brush the aubergine slices with olive oil then grill them on both sides either under the grill, or in a very hot grill pan. Make sure the aubergine is soft, evenly cooked and golden on each side.

Meanwhile, make the topping. Put the crème fraîche and the preserved mushrooms into a small saucepan and heat through very gently until just bubbling.

Arrange even numbers of cooked aubergine slices on 4 warmed plates. Sprinkle with a little lemon juice then smother with the hot sauce.

Sprinkle generously with the chopped parsley and a little pepper, garnish with lemon slices and sprigs of flat leaf parsley and serve immediately with a crisp green salad or a tomato salad.

Provatura is basically a Roman version of mozzarella. It is only made with buffalo milk and is about the size and shape of a large egg. It tends to be slightly more solid and creamy than mozzarella. If you cannot get hold of provatura, you can use scamorza, which is a matured mozzarella that is sometimes smoked. Otherwise, use fresh mozzarella that has been allowed to harden slightly over three or four days. This recipe is very useful for using up slightly dry mozzarella that is past its best. It's even more delicious when cooked over a barbecue.

grilled cheese with anchovy sauce
spiedini di provatura o scamorza

serves 4

300 g (10 oz) provatura or
scamorza cheese
1 small loaf coarse crusty bread
150 g (5 oz) unsalted butter
2 large salted anchovies, boned
and rinsed
2 tbsp milk
freshly ground black pepper

method

Cut the cheese and the bread into equal-sized discs of about 2 cm ($^3/_4$ inch).

Thread them alternately on to wooden skewers, making sure they are packed as tightly as possible. Grill or barbecue until the cheese is just running and the bread is crisp and toasted.

Meanwhile, put the butter and the anchovies into a small pan and warm over a low heat, stirring constantly until the anchovies have cooked down to a smooth cream.

Add the milk as the mixture begins to amalgamate then season with pepper.

Arrange the skewers on a serving platter, drizzle with the anchovy sauce and serve at once.

5.

sweet things
LA DOLCE VITA

There are not many desserts in the repertoire of Italian recipes, but those which do exist are very special. No sumptuous Italian feast would be complete without a sweet ending of some sort, even if it's just a bowl of beautiful fresh fruit. Here is a selection of desserts using fruit, chocolate, coffee and other delicious ingredients.

Make sure the coffee is really strong so that the flavour really comes through in the parfait. For the best results, use an Italian 100% Arabica coffee, made in an espresso pot or machine.

coffee ice cream parfait
semifreddo al caffé

serves 6

1 egg plus 5 egg yolks
200 g (7 oz) icing sugar
3 tbsp strong cold espresso coffee
6 sheets of gelatine
250 ml (9 fl oz) whipping cream,
sweetened with 2 tbsp icing sugar

TO DECORATE
whipped cream
coffee beans

method

Put the egg and the egg yolks in a bowl. Tip in the icing sugar and pour in the coffee. Place the bowl over a pan of simmering water and whisk together thoroughly for about 15 minutes.

Remove the bowl from the heat and whisk until cold, or for about another 15 minutes.

Put the sheet gelatine in a separate bowl and cover with cold water. Leave to soak until soft, then squeeze out the excess moisture until relatively dry. Put the gelatine back in the bowl and warm over a pan of hot water until dissolved.

Once the gelatine is liquefied, gradually stir it into the egg mixture with a wooden spoon. Whip the cream and sugar mixture until firm then fold into the egg mixture using a metal spoon.

Pour this mixture into 6 individual bowls and place in the coldest part of your refrigerator for about 1 hour until thoroughly chilled.

When you are ready to serve, decorate the top of each semifreddo with tufts of whipped cream and a few coffee beans. Serve with some light biscuits.

Use the best chocolate you can find for this recipe. Chocolate with a high cocoa content (70–80%) gives the richest flavour. Good-quality ice cream is also a must, and these days it's easy to come by.

decadent italian chocolate cake with ice cream
torta al cioccolato con il gelato

serves 6–8

175 g (6 oz) dark chocolate, 70% cocoa

150 g (5 oz) unsalted butter, cubed, plus extra for greasing

5 large eggs, separated

200 g (7 oz) caster sugar

1 tsp baking powder

2 tbsp cocoa powder

100 g (3½ oz) plain flour

about 8 tbsp softened vanilla or chocolate ice cream

icing sugar, for dusting

method

Preheat the oven to 180°C (350°F) Gas 4. Prepare a 20 cm (8 inch) loose-bottomed cake tin by lining with baking parchment and greasing with butter.

Chop the chocolate into bite-sized pieces and place in a heatproof bowl. Set the bowl over a pan of lightly simmering water and stir with a wooden spoon until it has melted. Add the butter and continue to stir until it has melted into the chocolate.

Meanwhile, beat the egg whites until stiff then slowly fold in the sugar.

In a separate bowl, mix the baking powder with the cocoa powder and flour.

Remove the chocolate mixture from the heat and stir in the egg yolks. When the egg yolks and chocolate are well combined, gently fold the mixture into the beaten egg whites.

Finally, sift in the flour and cocoa mixture and fold in with a large metal spoon.

Turn the mixture into the prepared tin and bake in the oven for 35 minutes or until the cake has slightly come away from the edges of the tin.

Remove the cake from the oven and leave to cool in the tin, then turn out on to a cooling rack.

Slice the cake in half. Spread the ice cream over one half then sandwich the cake back together. Serve at once dusted with icing sugar.

A very simple way to end a summer lunch or supper. You can also use peaches, nectarines, cherries or apricots. Walnut bread is especially good for these. Also delicious with fresh figs.

plum crostini
crostini di miele e prugne

serves 4–6

12 soft ripe plums
300 g (10 oz) ricotta cheese
12 small slices Italian bread,
preferably walnut
4 tbsp clear honey

method

Remove the stones from the plums and put the fruit into a blender. Whizz until you have a coarse purée then mix with the ricotta.

Toast the bread lightly and spread with half the honey. Pile the plum mixture on top of the toast then slide under a very hot grill for about 2 minutes or until the ricotta begins to brown slightly. Drizzle with the remaining honey and serve.

This recipe works best with slightly under-ripe nectarines. The combination of almonds and nectarines is wonderful. The best dessert wines to use for this dish are Marsala, Moscato or Malvasia – you won't need a whole bottle so you can serve the remaining wine, chilled, with the finished dessert.

baked nectarines with amaretti
pesche noci ripiene d'amaretti

serves 4

4 fairly hard nectarines
4 Amaretti biscuits, finely crumbled
30 g (1¼ oz) bitter cooking chocolate, grated
30 g (1¼ oz) granulated sugar
25 g (1 oz) blanched almonds, chopped
150 ml (¼ pint) sweet Sicilian dessert wine

method

Preheat the oven to 190°C (375°F) Gas 5.

Cut the nectarines in half and remove the stone. Scoop out about half of the flesh and mash it with the crumbled Amaretti, grated chocolate, sugar and almonds. Dampen the mixture with enough of the wine to make it sticky then divide it evenly between the halved fruits.

Arrange the filled nectarines in an ovenproof dish and surround with the remaining wine. Cover loosely with foil and bake in the oven for about 30 minutes or until the nectarines are tender, basting occasionally with the juices and wine.

Remove the foil and either raise the oven temperature until the fruits have crisped slightly, or slide them under a hot grill for about 5 minutes. Serve warm or cold.

I have given you a selection of citrus fruits which you can vary according to taste and availability. This is a perfect salad to follow a heavy main course and is ideal as a palate cleanser.

citrus fruit salad
insalata di agrumi

serves 6

1 large ruby or yellow grapefruit
1 large pink grapefruit
2 large oranges
2 or 3 seedless clementines
1 lemon
1 lime
3–4 tablespoons caster sugar
1–2 tablespoons Maraschino or
Cointreau (optional)

method

Carefully remove the skin and pith from the grapefruits and oranges. Cut through to the centre so that the segments can be removed while leaving behind all the skin and pips. Put the fruit in a bowl.

Now peel and separate the clementines into segments, pulling off as much pith as you can. Add them to the bowl.

Prepare the lemon and lime garnish. Wash the lemon and lime then slice as thinly as possible.

Stir 1–2 tablespoons of sugar into the fruit. Taste and add more sugar, if necessary. Stir in the Maraschino or Cointreau (if using).

Mix all the fruit together and arrange in stemmed glasses or in a pretty glass bowl to serve. Garnish with the lemon and lime slices. Chill thoroughly before serving.

This is especially good when made with peaches that are slightly under-ripe and served with very good-quality, rich vanilla ice cream.

peaches in white wine with ice cream
pesche al vino bianco col gelato

serves 4

4 yellow peaches
4 tbsp caster sugar
500 ml (17 fl oz) dry white wine
a handful of fresh mint leaves
4 large scoops of vanilla ice cream

method

Blanch the peaches in boiling water for 1 minute, then skin, stone and slice them thickly.

Put the peach slices in a bowl and sprinkle with the sugar. Mix together then cover them with the white wine. Add the mint and put in the fridge for 1 hour so the flavours have time to develop.

Remove the peaches from the fridge and drain. Arrange the fruit in 4 individual serving bowls, cover with ice cream and drizzle over any remaining wine to serve.

Individual little brioche buns are not only delicious but also very useful for creating quick desserts or sweet snacks. This neat dessert is ideal for picnics.

brioche with figs
brioche con i fichi

serves 4

4 small brioche buns
6 fresh ripe figs
4 tbsp fresh ricotta cheese
1 tbsp caster sugar

method

Split the brioche buns in half. Peel 4 of the figs and mash them with the ricotta and sugar. Slice the remaining 2 figs thinly.

Spread the ricotta and fig mixture inside the 4 buns, arrange a few slices of fig on top and sandwich them back together. Eat quickly!

It is hard to imagine improving upon the natural flavour of fresh figs, they are so incredibly delicious. They are also superb with Prosciutto and fantastic with salami. However, the flavours of dark rum and brown sugar, added to the luxury of cream, make a very special dessert out of this wonderful fruit.

fresh figs with rum and cream
fichi freschi con il rum e la panna

serves 4

12 fresh figs
5 tbsp dark rum
3 tbsp flaked almonds
6 tbsp extra-thick double cream
2 tbsp single cream
2 tsp soft brown sugar

method

Peel the figs very carefully so as not to break them up. Cut them in half and arrange them in a single layer in a shallow glass dish.

Pour the dark rum all over the figs then sprinkle over the almonds.

Mix the creams together thoroughly then carefully pour over the figs and almonds so as not to disperse the layers. Sprinkle with the soft brown sugar and chill until required.

A wonderfully easy and lovely-looking dessert. You can make your own profiteroles very easily or you can buy them ready-made, depending on how much time you have. You can vary the flavours of the ice cream to suit your taste, but I think chocolate, vanilla and pistachio is the perfect combination with the strawberry sauce.

profiteroles with ice cream
bigne al gelato

serves 6

FOR THE PROFITEROLES
250 ml (9 fl oz) water
100 g (3½ oz) salted butter
175 g (6 oz) plain flour
5 eggs
butter, for greasing

FOR THE FILLINGS AND SAUCE
200 g (7 oz) fresh strawberries
juice of 1 lemon
2 tbsp icing sugar
200 ml (7 fl oz) whipping cream
200 g (7 oz) vanilla ice cream
200 g (7 oz) pistachio ice cream
200 g (7 oz) chocolate ice cream
fresh mint leaves, for decorating

method

Preheat the oven to 180°C (350°F) Gas 4. Line a baking tray with baking parchment and butter it thoroughly.

To make the profiteroles, put the water in a large pan and add the butter and flour. Mix together until smooth, then place over a medium heat and stir thoroughly until the mixture forms a soft dough and comes away from the sides of the pan.

Turn the dough into a bowl and add the eggs, one at a time. Using an electric whisk, blend the eggs into the dough.

Pour the mixture into a piping bag then pipe 18 small balls of dough on to the greased baking parchment, ensuring that there is plenty of space between each one.

Bake in the oven for 20–25 minutes, then remove and carefully place the profiteroles on a rack to cool.

To make the sauce put the strawberries into the food processor with the lemon juice and icing sugar. Whizz until smooth, then pour into a bowl and set aside.

In a separate bowl, whip the cream until stiff then chill until required.

Carefully slice the profiteroles open with a sharp knife or pair of scissors. Generously fill 6 of the profiteroles with vanilla ice cream, 6 with pistachio ice cream and 6 with chocolate ice cream.

Arrange all the filled profiteroles on a large platter or in a pretty serving bowl and drizzle with the strawberry sauce. Decorate with the whipped cream and mint leaves then serve at once.

These delectable little tarts are made using crumbled Amaretti biscuits – the flavour of the almond biscuits and the ripe pears is delicious.

individual pear and amaretto tarts
crostatine di pere e amaretti

serves 6

250 g (9 oz) plain white flour, plus extra for dusting

100 g (3½ oz) caster sugar

100 g (3½ oz) unsalted butter, cubed, plus extra for greasing

1 egg, plus 1 egg yolk, beaten

2 tsp baking powder, sifted

1 tsp vanilla essence

a pinch of salt

3–4 tbsp apple and pear fruit spread

75 g (3 oz) Amaretti biscuits, crumbled

750 g (1 lb 10 oz) ripe pears, peeled and thinly sliced

50 g (2 oz) pine nuts

2 oz (50 g) caster sugar

milk, for brushing

icing sugar, for dusting

vanilla ice cream, to serve (optional)

method

Preheat the oven to 180°C (350°F) Gas 4. Butter 6 individual tart tins then dust with flour and breadcrumbs.

Pile all the flour on to a large clean work surface or pastry board. Make a hollow in the centre of the flour with your fist and pour in the sugar, butter, beaten eggs, baking powder, vanilla essence and salt. Knead all this together to make a soft dough, then roll into a ball.

Tear off or cut away one third of the dough and roll it into a ball. Roll the remaining dough into a ball and set both balls of dough aside until required.

Cover the bases of the prepared tart tins with a layer of apple and pear fruit spread. Now arrange a thick layer of the crushed Amaretti on top.

Roll out the larger ball of dough to make a sheet and use to line the tart tins. Arrange the pear slices on top then scatter over the pine nuts and caster sugar.

Roll the reserved ball of dough along with any trimmings from the first ball into thin sausage shapes. Arrange long pieces around the outside edges of the tarts. Use the remaining dough to make a lattice pattern on top of each tart.

Bake for 20–30 minutes or until well browned. Brush generously with plenty of milk, then bake for a further 10 minutes (this keeps the pastry nice and crumbly).

Take the tarts out of their tins and put each one on a flat plate. Dust lightly with a little icing sugar. Serve warm with a scoop of vanilla ice cream (if using).

This is an ideal way to use those end-of-season, slightly woolly peaches that have lost most of their juice. Apples or pears, or a combination of any of these fruits is also delicious. My favourite fruit is the quince, which you could also use, although being such a hard fruit, it would need pre-cooking before adding to the cake to make sure that it would be soft by the time the cake was baked!

peach cake
torta di pesche

serves 4

a little softened butter, for greasing
3 tbsp stale, plain biscuit crumbs
2 large eggs
150 g (5 oz) caster sugar
180 g (6½ oz) plain white flour, sifted
125 ml/4 fl oz milk
grated zest of ½ lemon
1 heaped tsp baking powder, sifted
1 kg (2¼ lb) peaches, sliced
50 g (2 oz) butter, cut into small pieces
2 tbsp granulated or light brown sugar

method

Preheat the oven to 180°C (350°F) Gas 4. Thoroughly grease a 25 cm (10 inch) cake tin with softened butter then dust with the biscuit crumbs. Turn the tin upside down to remove all the loose crumbs and discard them. Set the prepared tin aside until required.

Beat the eggs until light and fluffy.

Gradually add the caster sugar then fold in the flour, milk, lemon zest and baking powder. The mixture should be quite runny.

Pour the cake mixture into the prepared cake tin. Arrange the peaches over the top, dot with the pieces of butter and sprinkle over the granulated or light brown sugar.

Bake in the oven for 55 minutes or until the cake has slightly come away from the edges of the tin.

Remove the cake from the oven and cool completely on a wire rack. When cool, remove the cake from the tin and serve.

As I am not very good at making pastry and don't like fussy desserts, I like to make pies that are a little bit rough and ready like this one. Bought pastry makes it even quicker and easier, especially if it comes ready-rolled, but you can make your own sweet or shortcrust pastry if you prefer.

summer fruit pie
sfoglia di frutta estiva

serves 6

1 sheet ready-rolled shortcrust or sweet pastry

4 dry sweet biscuits (such as Marie or Morning Coffee), crumbled

4 nectarines, peaches or large apricots

6 apricots or plums

100 g (3½ oz) blueberries, cherries (stoned), strawberries, redcurrants or raspberries

1 egg white, beaten

1 tbsp granulated or demerara sugar

1 tbsp smooth apricot jam, mixed with 1 tbsp hot water

method

Preheat the oven to 200°C (400°F) Gas 6.

Place the pastry on to a sheet of non-stick parchment or paper and carefully roll out. (Some ready-to-use sheets of pastry can be bought ready-rolled on a sheet of baking paper.)

Scatter the crumbled biscuits down the middle of the sheet of pastry. Wash the fruit and remove the stones. Cut all the large fruit into segments, then pile all the fruit into the centre of the pastry and over the biscuits.

Fold the pastry back on itself to make a thick crust all the way around the fruit and biscuits but leaving it uncovered. Do this quickly, so that the pastry does not soften too much in the warmth of your hands.

Whisk the egg white with the sugar and brush this all over the pastry crust around the exposed fruit. Slide the pie into the freezer for 5 minutes to set the egg white and sugar glaze, or put it in the fridge for about 15 minutes.

Take the pie out of the fridge or freezer and slide it straight into the oven. Bake for 25 minutes.

Remove from the oven and brush the pastry crust with the diluted apricot jam for added shine. Serve warm or at room temperature, with vanilla ice cream.

A very easy but delicious tart that makes the most of some of summer's fruit bounty. You can vary the fruit as you wish using, for example, strawberries and peaches or bluebuerries and ripe pears. This is also a lovely teatime treat.

plum, raspberry and almond tart
crostata di prugne, lamponi e mandorle

serves 4–6

FOR THE PASTRY

250 g (9 oz) plain flour

50 g (2 oz) ground almonds

150 g (5 oz) caster sugar

150 g/5 oz unsalted butter

2 eggs, beaten

FOR THE FILLING

4 large plums

100 g (3½ oz) raspberries

2 large eggs

4 tbsp double cream

75 g (3 oz) caster sugar

100 g (3½ oz) ground almonds

a handful of flaked almonds

butter, for greasing

a little icing sugar, for dusting

method

Put, the flour, almonds, caster sugar, butter and eggs in a large bowl or food processor. Mix together thoroughly with your fingertips or in the food processor until a firm dough forms.

Wrap the dough in clingfilm and chill until needed. Remember that overworking pastry makes it heavy and brittle. You could also buy ready-made sweet pastry if you don't want to make your own.

Preheat the oven to 180°C (350°F) Gas 4 and grease a 23 cm (9 inch) tart tin with the butter.

Stone the plums and slice them into segments. Wash the raspberries and remove any that are damaged.

Roll out the pastry and line the tart tin evenly with it. Arrange the fruit around the base of the pastry case, starting from the centre and working towards the edges.

Beat together the eggs, cream, sugar and ground almonds to make a custard then pour it over the fruit. Sprinkle with the flaked almonds.

Bake in the oven until the custard has set (about 20 minutes). Remove from the oven and leave to cool. Carefully remove the tart from the tin and place on a serving plate. Dust with icing sugar just before serving.

This is a deliciously crumbly, sumptuous tart which can be made using apricots or peaches or plums, all of which can be either fresh or dried. I like to serve it with a dollop of very fresh mascarpone on the side. You can also make it as individual tartlets if you prefer.

apricot and almond tart
crostata d'albicocche e mandorle

serves 6

method

FOR THE PASTRY
100 g (3½ oz) unsalted butter
200 g (7 oz) plain flour
50 g (2 oz) caster sugar
1 egg plus 1 egg yolk
grated zest of 1 unwaxed lemon

FOR THE FILLING
200 g (7 oz) ried or fresh apricots
100 ml (3½ fl oz) brandy
200 g (7 oz) unsalted butter
175 g (6 oz) caster sugar
200 g (7 oz) flaked blanched almonds
2 eggs
1 heaped tbsp plain flour
icing sugar, to dust

Preheat the oven to 200°C (400°F) Gas 6 and grease a 25 cm (10 inch) loose-bottomed tart tin.

Rub the butter into the flour then add the sugar. Bind the mixture together with the egg, egg yolk and lemon zest. Form into a ball then wrap in cling film and rest for an hour in the fridge.

Take the pastry out of the refrigerator and roll it out so it is large enough to line the tart tin. Trim off any excess and put the lined tin in the refrigerator for 15 minutes, or in the freezer for 5 minutes.

Line the chilled pastry with baking parchment and add some baking beans, or dried beans such as kidney beans, and bake blind for about 12 minutes. Test to see if the pastry is crisp and dry; if it is too wet, remove the paper and bake for a further 5 minutes.

Remove the pastry from the oven, reduce the heat to 180°C (350°F) Gas 4 and allow the pastry case to cool.

Meanwhile, poach the fruit in the brandy over a gentle heat for about 5 minutes, then leave to cool.

In the food processor, whizz together the butter and sugar until pale and fluffy. Add the almonds, eggs and flour and blend quickly.

Spoon this mixture into the pastry case and cover it with the poached fruit. Bake in the oven for 30–40 minutes or until golden brown.

Check the tart from time to time and if it seems to be getting too brown on the top, cover it loosely with foil.

Remove the tart from the oven, allow to cool, then transfer on to a platter. When cold and just before serving, sprinkle with icing sugar to decorate.

A semifreddo is almost an ice cream, but not quite. This is a very light, easy and pretty dessert that is good to enjoy at the end of a long lazy lunch on the terrace or in the garden. You can use any berry you like.

raspberry semifreddo
semifreddo di lamponi

serves 4

14 large boudoir biscuits (Savoiardi) or
20 smaller biscuits
2 tbsp raspberry or strawberry jam
2 tbsp medium dry sherry or
dessert wine
juice of 1 lemon
250 g (9 oz) raspberries or other
berries, plus extra for decorating
40 g (1½ oz) caster sugar
200 ml (7 fl oz) fresh whipping cream
2 egg whites, chilled

method

Cut the biscuits in half through the centres and spread with the jam. Line the base and sides of a 1 litre (1¾ pint) mould with the biscuits then drizzle with the sherry or dessert wine to moisten.

Put the lemon juice and the berries in a food processor with the sugar. Whizz until smooth then sieve to remove all the seeds. Pour the purée into a bowl.

Whip the cream and fold it into the raspberry purée. Beat the chilled egg whites until really stiff and gently fold them into the mixture.

Fill the biscuit-lined mould with the fruit mousse then place the filled mould on a tray. Put it in the freezer to set for at least 2 hours.

To serve, dip the mould into hot water for 10 seconds, then turn the semifreddo out on to a plate, decorate with a few berries and serve at once.

An alternative version of the classic chilled zabaglione that is perfect for those chillier evenings on the terrace! Served warm, it is a wonderfully comforting but grown-up dessert.

spiced zabaglione with red wine
zabaglione alle spezie con il vino rosso

serves 4

4 egg yolks
4 tbsp red wine
4 tbsp caster sugar
a large pinch of ground cinnamon
a large pinch of ground ginger
a large pinch of ground nutmeg
a large pinch of ground cloves

method

Beat all the ingredients in a large heatproof bowl and whisk together using a balloon whisk.

Place the bowl over a double boiler or a pan of simmering water, making sure the water never touches the bowl containing the egg mixture.

Using an electric whisk, beat the egg mixture until light and fluffy and the mixture leaves a thick trail when allowed to drop from the whisk.

Pour into 4 stemmed glasses and serve at once with some Cantuccini biscuits. It's much better served warm!

This is a slight twist on the classic recipe, with the caramel adding another dimension to the flavour. Please make sure the Mascarpone is really fresh for the best results and let the tiramisu stand for as long as possible before serving. Italian Savoiardi biscuits are the best type to use as they are much softer and more absorbent.

Valentina's classic tiramisu with caramel
il tiramisu classico con il caramello

serves 4–6

250 g (9 oz) Mascarpone or very rich cream cheese
4 eggs, separated
4 tbsp caster sugar
2 tsp strong espresso coffee
4 tbsp granulated or caster sugar
100 g/3½ oz bitter cooking chocolate, broken into small pieces
8 tbsp weak coffee
6 tbsp rum, brandy, Tia Maria or other liqueur
about 20 Savoiardi biscuits (sponge fingers)
2 tsp cocoa powder
2 tsp instant coffee powder

method

Whisk the cheese until soft and manageable. Beat the egg yolks until pale then whisk them into the cheese.

Very gradually add the caster sugar to the cheese mixture, stirring and whisking constantly. Pour in the espresso coffee and mix thoroughly.

Melt the granulated or caster sugar in a small pan until liquid and brown then pour it on to a lightly oiled surface. Allow it to harden completely, then break into small pieces using a hammer wrapped in clingfilm. Collect up all the pieces of caramel and stir them into the cheese mixture.

Beat the egg whites until very stiff then fold them into the cheese mixture. Mix the chocolate gently into the mixture.

Next, mix together the weak coffee and the liqueur. Dip half the sponge biscuits into the coffee mixture one at a time and use them to line the bottom of a serving bowl. Pour over half the cheese mixture.

Dip the remaining biscuits in the coffee liquid and layer in the bowl, covering the cheese layer. Pour over the remaining cheese mixture . Bang the dish down lightly to settle the layers.

Mix the cocoa powder and coffee powder and sieve over the dessert. Chill for at least 3 hours, preferably overnight.

The flavour of cinnamon is incredibly intense and surprisingly refreshing. This light dessert looks especially attractive when served on top of a vine leaf and decorated with edible flowers. You'll need to plan ahead if you want to make it though, as the cinnamon sticks take 12 hours to infuse in the water.

cinnamon jelly
gelo di cannella

serves 6

10 g (¼ oz) cinnamon sticks
750 ml (1¼ pints) cold water
300 g (10 oz) caster sugar
60 g (2½ oz) cornflour
50 g (2 oz) cooking chocolate
lemon leaves, to decorate

method

Put the cinnamon sticks and cold water into a pan. Place over a medium heat and bring to the boil, then boil gently for about 5 minutes. Remove from the heat and leave to stand for 12 hours.

Strain the cinnamon liquid carefully and return to the pan. Add the sugar. Dissolve the cornflour in 2 tablespoons of the cinnamon liquid then pour back into the pan. Bring the liquid to the boil, stirring constantly, and simmer very gently until thickened.

Remove the pan from the heat and add the chocolate, stirring until it has melted. Turn into 1 large or 6 individual moulds and chill until solid. Turn out and decorate with lemon leaves to serve.

ALTERNATIVE

• If you prefer a clearer jelly, you can use 3 sheets of gelatine or powdered gelatine (follow instructions on the packet) instead of the cornflour. In this case, you should add the gelatine to the liquid after you have strained it and returned it to the boil.

index